To
Victor Remington
Happy Collecting 5/25/76
Gail Krause

THE ENCYCLOPEDIA OF DUNCAN GLASS

The Encyclopedia of Duncan Glass

Gail Krause

ILLUSTRATED

Exposition Press   *Hicksville, New York*

To all the people whose love, efforts, and talents produced "The Loveliest Glassware in America." To Bill Meeks for his photography, and to the following for permitting us to photograph their collections: James Davis, Betty Dimmack, John Grummick, Walter "Dutch" Jones, Joseph Kapis, James Lowery, Earl Meeks, Patrick Morris, J. Wilson McCarl, E. M. Viehmann, Gerald Thompson and Glenn Strawn.

Very special thanks to my husband, Jack, for the encouragement and patience given me while writing this book. Had it not been for him and all the others contributing their time, knowledge and assistance, this book might never have been completed.

FIRST EDITION

© 1976 by Gail Krause

Copyright © under the Universal Copyright and Berne Conventions

ISBN 0-682-48527-6

Printed in the United States of America

CONTENTS

INTRODUCTION

It is with pride that I present to you this encyclopedia of Duncan glass. The skill, artistry, and knowledge required to produce an item of "The Loveliest Glassware in America" speak for themselves. Many of the women and men are still living and have provided me with many facts from the past and an incentive for future collecting. On the following pages are photographs, catalog page reprints, and illustrations to identify patterns of glassware and crystal.

We the collectors living in Washington, Pennsylvania, are fortunate to have been a little closer to the people and to the factory that produced this glass for 62 of the years this company existed.

The story began in 1865 when George Duncan bought out Ripley and Company located on Tenth and Carson Streets, Pittsburgh, Pennsylvania. Prior to this, he and Daniel C. Ripley had worked together manufacturing bar glasses and flint glassware.

Harry B. and James E. Duncan, Sr., joined their father, along with Augustus H. Heisey, the son-in-law who had married George's daughter Susan. It was a difficult period for many as the country was to experience the effects of the forthcoming Depression of 1870.

It was a wise move on the part of George Duncan, as Augustus Heisey became very well known, and many early patterns were attributed to him. He founded his own factory in 1895, which existed until 1957 in Newark, Ohio.

Another man destined to establish a great name for himself for the firm was John Ernest Miller, who became famous the world over for his designs. The outstanding one was the "Three Face" pattern, where one full face and two profiles could be seen on the stem, regardless of the position. The model for this particular design was his lovely wife, Elizabeth Blair Miller. The first piece, a cake plate, was said to have been awarded one of the prizes at the Centennial Exposition in Philadelphia, Pennsylvania. Later, many other articles were made in this pattern, such as lamps, compotes, water goblets, wines, and the like.

George Duncan & Sons joined the United States Glass Company in a glass trust in 1891 and dissolved their association when fire destroyed the Duncan plant in 1892.

Washington, Pennsylvania, was looking for new industry, and the

Duncans decided to locate their new plant on Jefferson Avenue. The factory was completed in January, but the first glassware was not run until February 9, 1893, in a 16 pot deep eye furnace. The first pattern reportedly made at that time was the Mitchell pattern. The company was incorporated in 1900 with the following: Mrs. Anna Duncan, Mr. James E. Duncan, Mr. Andrew P. Duncan, Mr. Harry Duncan, and Mr. J. Ernest Miller, and was named The Duncan & Miller Glass Company.

The company continued making fine glassware, which was shipped the world over, until one day the foremen and the union officials were told that the plant was to be sold. Some of the molds and the equipment were sold to the United States Glass Company in Tiffin, Ohio, which was to continue making ware under a "Duncan & Miller Division" as a separate operation of their plant.

Many of the former workers of Duncan had already been sent to Tiffin to set up operations and to show how some of their color combinations and some of their swans and other articles were made.

The Duncan & Miller Glass Company tried to place as many of their employees as possible in surrounding glass plants. It was a sad day for all concerned. Some of the people felt they were too old to change employment and take up roots in a strange city. Some went to Tiffin, Ohio, and others to Glassport, Pennsylvania. Once again machines had replaced men in doing a job. The Duncans bowed to progress; they simply could no longer afford to have 10 to 14 men make one swan or article. Although the closing date of the factory was June 24, 1955, the 14 pot furnace was not turned off until August 30, 1955. The company had buyers looking at the plant; also, orders had to be completed. The stock on hand was sold to the public at fantastic bargains. The cutters were among the last people to leave the plant, it has been told. Many of these people went to Tiffin, Ohio, New Martinsville, West Virginia, and sought other employment.

Andy Brothers of Washington, Pennsylvania, a company that recapped tires, had bought the building and had not yet moved completely into it when fire destroyed the ex-factory on June 29, 1956. Hundreds of people watched as the fire gutted the old building, and the flames could be seen for miles around.

So ends that chapter of the Duncan story, but a new chapter begins as we collectors protect and preserve this fine ware that has survived for over a century.

THE ENCYCLOPEDIA OF DUNCAN GLASS

DUNCAN & MILLER PATTERNS

AMERICAN WAY

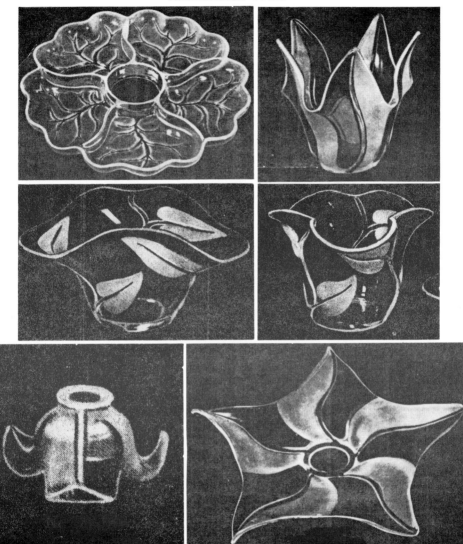

CRYSTAL

Satintone Finish

First row: (left and right) No. 78-C 15 in. 6-compartment hors d'oeuvre, height—1½ in.; No. 72-E 8 in. flared vase. *Second row:* (left and right) No. 71-W 12½ in. oval bowl, height—5½ in., width—8 in.; No. 71-T 6½ in. cloverleaf vase. *Third row:* (left and right) No. 71-D 2 in. candlestick; No. 76-A 14 in. star-shaped plate.

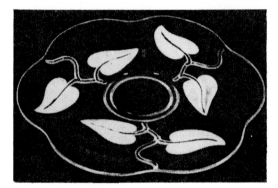

First row: (left and right) No. 71½-A 8 in. 3-compartment candy box and cover, height—3¾ in.; No. 71-A 9½ in. flared vase. *Second row:* (center) No. 71-E 14 in. plate with flat edge, also made with rolled edge (No. 71-F). *Third row:* (left and right) No. 71½-G 7½ in. low-footed, flared comport, height—5 in.; No. 71-M 12 in. crimped centerpiece, height—4¾ in.

ASTAIRE*

No. 22 Pattern

Above: (left to right) goblet; 8½ in. plate; 6 in. footed bonbon; finger bowl and plate; 12 oz. iced tea. *Below:* (left to right) 5 oz. parfait; 5 oz. saucer champagne; 5 oz. footed ice cream; 3 oz. wine; 3 oz. cocktail; 1 oz. cordial; 9 oz. tumbler; 7 oz. old-fashioned cocktail; 5 oz. orange juice; 2 oz. tumbler.

*See color photo section.

CANTERBURY*

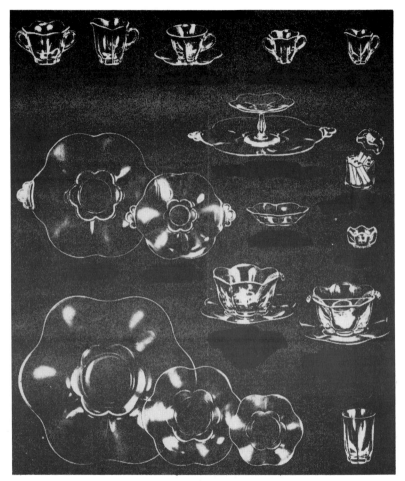

No. 115 Pattern

First row: (left to right) 7 oz. sugar; 7 oz. cream; teacup and saucer; 3 oz. individual sugar; 3 oz. individual cream. *Second row:* (left to right) 11 in. 2-handled plate; 7½ in. 2-handled plate; 5 in. fruit nappy; 3 in. ashtray; (background, left and right) 11 in. 2-handled cheese and cracker set; cigarette jar and cover. *Third row:* (left to right) 14 in. plate; 8 in. plate; 6 in. plate; 9 oz. tumbler; (background, left and right) 3 pc. mayonnaise set: mayonnaise bowl; 8½ in. plate, ladle; 4 pc. twin mayonnaise set: 2-compartment mayonnaise bowl; 8½ in. plate, two ladles.

---

*See color photo section.

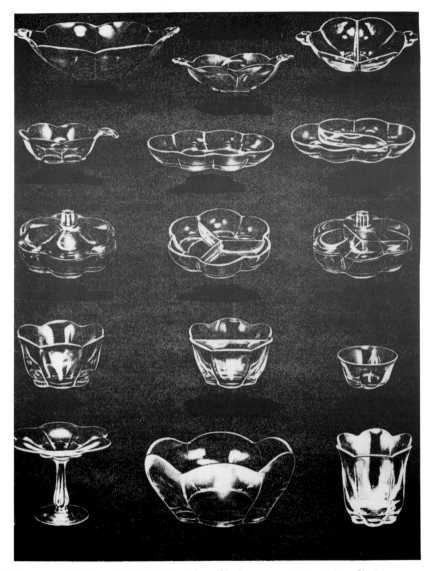

First row: (left to right) 9 in. 2-handled nappy; 6 in. 2-handled nappy; 6 in. 2-handled, 2-compartment relish. *Second row:* (left to right) 5 in. single-handled nappy; 8 in. pickle tray; 8 in. 2-compartment pickle and olive tray. *Third row:* (left to right) 7 in. candy box and cover; 7 in. 3-compartment relish; 7 in. 3-compartment candy box and cover. *Fourth row:* (left to right) mayonnaise; 2-compartment mayonnaise or salad-dressing bowl; finger bowl. *Fifth row:* (left to right) 6 in. high-footed comport; 10 in. salad bowl; 5 in. ice bucket.

First row: (left and right) 12 in. flared bowl; 12 in. oval bowl. *Second row:* (left to right) 3-light candlestick, height—6 in., width—10 in.; 3 in. candlestick; 6 in. candlestick. *Third row:* (left to right) 3-light candelabrum with U prisms, height—7 in., width—11 in., 3 bobeches; 1-light candelabrum with U prisms, height—7 in.; 3-light candelabrum with U prisms, height—7 in., width—11 in., 2 bobeches. *Fourth row:* (left to right) 8 in. vase; 12 in. vase; 4½ in. rose bowl.

LEAD BLOWN STEMWARE
No. 5115 Pattern

First row: (left to right) 10 oz. goblet; 5 oz. saucer champagne; 5 oz. claret; 3 oz. liquor cocktail; 3½ oz. wine. *Second row:* (left to right) 1 oz. cordial; 5 oz. footed ice cream; 4 oz. oyster cocktail. *Third row:* (left to right) 12 oz. footed iced tea; 10 oz. footed tumbler; 5 oz. footed orange juice; finger bowl.

CANTERBURY

Duncan & Miller's Canterbury was created during the Second World War, when there was a shortage of fine crystal being imported. Our country needed more important items for the war effort, which led to the ingenuity of these great craftsmen.

They designed a pattern that would be suited for the modern trends or could be blended with Old World formality. Few designs can compare with this particular one. The clear, flowing lines, the simplicity, the flawless beauty make this one of the most popular patterns. Some of these items were also produced in pink and blue opalescent. 9 in. 2-handled opalescence; 6 in. 2-handled nappy; 6 in. 2-handled 2-compartment relish; single-handled nappy; individual cream and sugar; 8 in. 2-compartment pickle and olive tray; 7 in. candy box and cover; 7 in. 3-compartment relish; 7 in. 3-compartment relish with cover (called candy box); 4½ in. rose bowl; cigarette box and cover; 8 in. vase.

The candy box and cigarette box and cover also came in blue crystal. The 7 in. candy box and the 7 in. 3-compartment candy box were also very popular in ruby.

This particular line was also a favorite blank for First Love, Adoration, and Language of Flowers.

CARIBBEAN*

This pattern was made in crystal and in light blue. Some of the pieces made in crystal, such as relish trays and punch cups, had colored handles in ruby, green, or amber. Duncan & Miller also made other items in this pattern: 12 in. round flower bowl; 8 in. candelabrum with prisms and bobeches (also available as candlesticks· without prisms and bobeches); 5-compartment relish dish, height—12¾ in., width—11 in.; oval bowl, height—5½ in.; cruet bottles with clear or ruby stoppers, height—3½ in.

---

*See color photo section.

COLONIAL

No. 54 Pattern

First row: (left to right) 1 oz. small salt and pepper, noncorrosive top; 1½ oz. medium salt and pepper, noncorrosive top; salted almond, height —2¾ in.; No. 54½ 3½ oz. mustard and cover; 8 in. spoon tray; No. 54½ 5½ oz. footed ice cream, height—3¾ in. *Second row:* (left to right) 9 oz. goblet; 5 oz. custard or punch cup; No. 54½ 4½ in. nappy; 4½ in. large finger bowl, 6¾ in. large finger bowl plate; 3½ in. small finger bowl, 6 in. small finger bowl plate; No. 54¾ 8 oz. footed ice cream, height—5 in. *Third row:* (left to right) 14 oz. hotel sugar; 10 oz. hotel cream; 3 oz. individual sugar; 2 oz. individual cream; No. 54½ 7 oz. Berry sugar; No. 54½ 4½ oz. Berry cream. *Fourth row:* (left to right) footed grapefruit, 5 oz. footed grapefruit liner; 16 oz. sugar and cover; 11 oz. cream; 10 oz. Berry sugar and cover; 8 oz. Berry cream. *Fifth row:* (left to right) carnation vase, height—9¾ in.; sweet pea vase, height—9 in.; qt. pitcher, also made in 3 pt. and ½ gal. sizes; pt. pitcher.

DIAMOND

No. 75 Pattern

First row: (left to right) 7 in. 2-handled crimped sweetmeat; 9 oz. goblet; 6 oz. saucer champagne; 3½ oz. wine; 3½ oz. cocktail; 6½ in. 2-handled, 2-compartment flared bonbon. *Second row:* (left to right) 4 pc. 6 in. twin salad-dressing set: 6 in. flared, twin salad-dressing bowl, 7½ in. 2-handled round plate, 2 mayonnaise ladles; 7 in. 2-handled oval pickle; 4½ in. 2-handled violet vase; 13 in. plate, rolled edge; *Third row:* (left to right) 8½ in. salad plate; 5 in. flower arranger; 8 in. sweet pea bowl; 8 in. 2-handled oval lemon plate; (background, left and right) 6½ in. 2-handled oval olive; 6 in. candy box and cover.

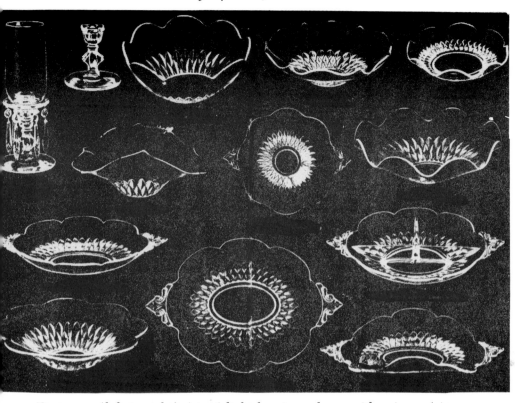

First row: (left to right) 4 in. 1-light hurricane lamp with prisms; 4 in. 1-light candlestick; 9½ in.-deep salad bowl; 9½ in. round bowl; 8 in. crimped bowl. *Second row:* (left to right) 10 in. oval bowl; 7½ in. 2-handled round plate; 11½ in. crimped bowl. *Third row:* (left to right) 11 in. 2-handled oval centerpiece; (center) 12 in. 2-handled oblong sandwich plate; 11 in. 2-handled, 3-compartment celery and relish. *Fourth row:* (left and right) 11½ in. flared bowl; 11 in. 2-handled muffin tray.

DUNCAN CUTTINGS

There is probably no operation in the whole varied process of glass-making which so many people have actually seen as cutting glass. Yet few of those who see the work actually realize how much skill is required.

When the design is being cut into a thin glass goblet, where the entire thickness of the glass is only one-sixteenth of an inch, it is very easy for an unskilled operator to cut through.

Great skill is required in the men who cut glass on these wheels, and a good glass cutter is really an artist.

Gray Cuttings. The cutting operation leaves a satiny finish on the glass. This is sometimes desirable as part of the pattern and is allowed to remain. Glass cut in this manner is known as GRAY CUT.

Rock-Crystal Cuttings. Where a glistening, clear crystal cutting is desired, the gray finish is removed by dipping the glass into a bath of acid. Glass finished in this way is known as ROCK CRYSTAL.

Duncan produces the Lovelace and Eternally Yours cuttings to harmonize with 1847 Rogers Bros. sterling silver patterns of the same names.

EARLY AMERICAN SANDWICH*

LACE GLASS
No. 41 Pattern

First row: (left to right) 9 oz. goblet; 3 pc. 13 in. salad-dressing set: 13 in. plate with ring, mayonnaise bowl, ladle; footed mayonnaise. *Second row:* (center) 12 in. plate. *Third row:* (left to right) candy jar and cover; 5 oz. orange juice; 10 in. footed vase.

---

*See color photo section.

First row: (left to right) 9 oz. goblet; 5 oz. saucer champagne; 3 oz. wine; 3 oz. cocktail; 5 oz. ice cream; 5 oz. flared sundae; 12 oz. footed iced tea; 9 oz. footed tumbler. *Second row:* (left to right) 6 in. low-footed comport; 6 in. low-footed flared comport; 12 in. lily bowl; teacup and saucer; finger bowl and plate. *Third row:* (left to right) 6 in. fruit salad; 6 in. grapefruit; 5 in. fruit nappy; 6 in. dessert nappy. *Fourth row:* (left to right) 12 in. ice cream tray with rolled edge; 12 in. 3-compartment relish; 12 in. chop plate with flat edge. *Fifth row:* (left to right) 9½ in. service or dinner plate; 8 in. salad plate; 7 in. dessert plate; 6 in. bread and butter plate; 5 in. coaster or plate.

First row: (left to right) 5 in. 3-light candlestick, height—7 in., width—
9 in.; 5 in. 3-light candelabrum, height—7 in., width—10 in., stubby
prisms; 4 in. 1-light candelabrum, stubby prisms; 5 in. 2-light candelabrum, height—5 in., width—10 in., stubby prisms; 5 in. 2-light candlestick, height—5 in., width—9 in. *Second row:* (left to right) 12 in. urn
and cover; 10 in. 3-compartment oblong relish; 10½ in. oblong camelia
flower pan; 10½ in. 3-compartment oblong celery and relish. *Third row:*
(left to right) urn; 10 in. celery tray; 12 in. shallow salad bowl; 10 in.
3-compartment fruit bowl for serving 3 kinds of canned fruit. *Fourth
row:* (left to right) 13 in. footed cake salver, flat edge; 12 in. footed cake
salver, rolled edge; 11½ in. crimped flower bowl. *Fifth row:* (left to right)
11½ in. crimped, footed fruit bowl; 11 in. flared, footed fruit bowl; 12 in.
footed oval fruit basket.

First row: (left to right) 5 in. candy box and cover; 7 in. pickle tray; 7 in. 2-compartment oblong relish; 5 in. footed bonbon and cover. *Second row:* (left to right) 5 in. footed ivy bowl; 6 oz. fruit cup or Jell-O; 3 in. footed cigarette holder; 5 oz. oyster cocktail; 7 in. low, flared candy comport. *Third row:* (left to right) 5 in. footed, fan-shaped vase, also made in 3 in. size; 8 in. oval tray; 6½ in. handled candy basket, also made in 5½ in. size; 2 pc. 6 in. shrimp or crabmeat service. *Fourth row:* (left to right) 5 in. crimped, footed vase, also made in 3 in. size; 3 pc. 5 oz. sugar and cream set: sugar, cream, 8 in. oval tray; 7 in. low, crimped candy comport; 5½ in. tall comport; 5½ in. grapefruit with rim liner or large frozen-fruit server. *Fifth row:* (left to right) 5 in. flared, footed vase, also made in 3 in. size; 5½ in. grapefruit with fruit cup liner; 5 pc. oil-and-vinegar condiment set: 3 oz. oil bottle, 3 oz. vinegar bottle, salt and pepper with glass top, 8 in. oval tray; 5½ in. low, crimped comport. *Sixth row:* (left to right) 4 pc. 6 in. twin salad-dressing set: 2-compartment salad-dressing bowl, 8 in. plate with rim, 2 glass or chromium ladles; 2 pc. 6 in. mayonnaise set: 6 in. footed mayonnaise bowl, glass or chromium ladle; 3 pc. 6 in. twin salad-dressing set: 2-compartment salad-dressing bowl, 2 glass or chromium ladles; 3 pc. 6 in. mayonnaise set: 6 in. footed mayonnaise bowl, 8 in. plate with rim, glass or chromium ladle.

First row: (left to right) individual ashtrays; cigarette box and cover; individual ashtrays. *Second row:* (left to right) 5 in. handled nappy, regular, also made in 6 in. size; 5 in. handled 2-compartment relish, also made in 6 in. size; 5 in. heart-shaped, handled bonbon, also made in 6 in. size; 6 in. handled mint tray, also made in 7 in. size. *Third row:* (left to right) 5½ in. cheese stand; 9 oz. sugar; 7 oz. cream; 5 in. 2-compartment nappy, also made in 6 in. size; 5 in. fruit nappy, also made in 6 in. size. *Fourth row:* (left to right) 2 pc. 13 in. cheese and cracker set; 3 pc. mayonnaise set: footed mayonnaise, 7 in. plate, ladle; 11 in. cupped nut bowl. *Fifth row:* (left to right) 12 in. flared fruit bowl; 8 in. butter or cheese and cover; 2 pc. salad set: 10 in. salad bowl, 13 in. plate.

First row: (left to right) 4 in. candlestick; 12 in. oblong bowl; 4 in. candlestick. *Second row:* (left and right) No. 1-C-41 3-light candelabrum with U prisms, height—16 in., width—13 in., 3 bobeches; No. 1-B-41 3-light candelabrum with U prisms, height—10 in., width—13 in., 2 bobeches. *Third row:* (left to right) No. 1-41 1-light candelabrum with U prisms, height—10 in.; 12 in. oblong bowl; No. 1-41 1-light candelabrum with U prisms, height—10 in.

ETERNALLY YOURS

HANDCUT ROCK CRYSTAL

First row: (left and right) No. 8 7½ in. tall comport; No. 41 2-light candlestick. *Second row:* (left to right) No. 30½ 10½ in. salad bowl, No. 33 13 in. plate; No. 30 8 in. flared, flip vase; No. 30 13 in. oval bowl; (foreground) No. 6 12 in. flared flower bowl. *Third row:* (left to right) No. 41 2-light candlestick; No. 30 12 in. 3-compartment relish; No. 5200 6 in. candy box and cover. *Fourth row:* (left to right) No. 31½ 12 in. 5-compartment relish; No. 30 11 in. 2-handled sandwich plate; No. 25 11 in. cheese and cracker set.

STEMWARE

No. 5331 Pattern

First row: (left to right) 6 oz. ice cream; 5 oz. fruit juice; 4½ oz. oyster cocktail; 3½ oz. liquor cocktail. *Second row:* (left to right) 6 oz. saucer champagne; 1 oz. cordial; 2 oz. sherry; 3 oz. wine. *Third row:* (left to right) 5 oz. claret; 10 oz. footed tumbler; 10 oz. goblet; 13 oz. footed iced tea.

FESTIVE

HANDMADE AND FLAME POLISHED
No. 155 Pattern

Clockwise: (from top right) No. 155/61 14 in. flower arranger; No. 155/31 9½ in. handled twin server or ashtray; No. 155/43 3 pc. sugar and cream service; No. 155/60 5½ in. candlestick; No. 155/32 10 in. handled, 3-compartment relish. (Colors: aqua, honey, or crystal)

Clockwise: (from top left) No. 155/30 8½ in. sauce bowl and ladle; No. 155/50 7½ in. comport; No. 155/51 8 in. candy box and cover; No. 155/33 15 in. oblong cheese service; No. 155/41 4 in. pepper; No. 155/40 4 in. salt; No. 155/42 8 in. cruet; No. 155/34 16 in. round buffet service. (Colors: aqua, honey, or crystal)

FIRST LOVE

ETCHED

First row: (left to right) No. 41 5 in. 2-light candlestick, also made as candelabra with bobeches and prisms; No. 41 5 in. 3-light candelabra with prisms, also made as candlestick without bobeches and prisms; No. 117 8 in. cornucopia vase, also made in 4 in. size; No. 126 11 in. footed, square-shaped vase. *Second row:* (left to right) No. 126 14 in. oval bowl; No. 126 10 in. footed, scalloped bowl; No. 111 12 in. footed, flared bowl. *Third row:* (left to right) No. 30 2-light candlestick; No. 111 11 in. flared bowl; No. 30 2-light candlestick; No. 111 9 in. deep salad bowl. *Fourth row:* (left to right) No. 117 candlestick or vase; No. 117 12 in. oval flower bowl; No. 117 4 in. candlestick or vase; No. 6 12 in. flared flower bowl. (Matches 1847 Rogers Bros. First Love silverplate)

First row: (left to right) No. 5111½ 10 oz. tall goblet; No. 5111½ 5 oz. saucer champagne; No. 5111½ 5 oz. ice cream; No. 5111½ 3½ oz. liquor cocktail; No. 5111½ 3 oz. wine; No. 5111½ 1 oz. cordial. *Second row:* (left to right) No. 5111½ 12 oz. footed iced tea; No. 5111½ 10 oz. low luncheon goblet; No. 5111½ 5 oz. footed orange juice; No. 5111½ 4½ oz. oyster cocktail; (background) No. 5111½ finger bowl. *Third row:* (left to right) No. 111 7 in. square nappy, also made in 5½ in. size; No. 5200 14 oz. tumbler, sham, also made in 5, 7, 10, 12, 16, and 18 oz. sizes; No. 5200 3½ oz. cocktail tumbler, sham; No. 5200 1½ oz. whiskey or cordial tumbler, sham; No. 5200 32 oz. decanter and stopper, also made in 16 oz. size. *Fourth row:* (left to right) No. 111 8½ in. round salad plate, also made in 6 and 7 in. sizes; No. 111 7½ in. square salad plate, also made in 6 in. size; No. 5200 32 oz. cocktail shaker with metal top, also made in 8 and 18 oz. sizes; No. 30 6 in. ice bucket with chrome handle and tongs.

First row: (top to bottom) No. 111 11 in. flared flower bowl; No. 111 10 in. footed vase; No. 111 13 in. torte plate with flat edge, also made with rolled edge. *Second row:* (top to bottom) No. 111 3 pc. mayonnaise set: 5½ in. footed and handled mayonnaise, ladle, plate; No. 111 11 in. shallow salad bowl; No. 111 10 in. 2-handled nappy; No. 111 sugar and cream; No. 111 4 in. low candlestick. *Third row:* (top to bottom) No. 5202 80 oz. jug, ice lip; No. 111 9 in. 2-handled, 4-compartment relish; No. 111 11 in. 2-handled cheese and cracker set; No. 111 11 in. 2-handled sandwich plate.

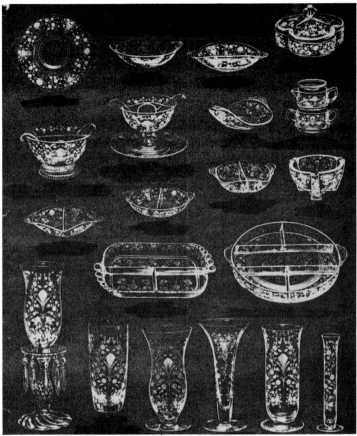

First row: (left to right) No. 111 6 in. 2-handled lemon plate; No. 111 6 in. 2-handled, regular-shaped nappy; No. 111 8 in. 2-handled celery tray; No. 106 6 in. 3-compartment candy box and cover. *Second row:* (left to right) No. 111 3 pc. 6 in. flared, 2-compartment salad-dressing set: 2-compartment salad-dressing bowl, 2 glass ladles; No. 30 4 pc. 5½ in. 2-compartment salad-dressing set: 2 compartment salad-dressing bowl, plate, 2 glass ladles; No. 111 6 in. 2-handled, basket-shaped nappy; No. 28 3 pc. breakfast set: sugar, cream, butter plate (nested). *Third row:* (left to right) No. 111 6 in. 2-handled, 2-compartment, diamond-shaped relish; No. 111 6 in. 2-handled, 2-compartment, round-shaped relish; No. 111 6 in. 2-handled, 2-compartment, square-shaped relish; No. 12 5 in. club ashtray, also made in 4 in. size. *Fourth row:* (center and right) No. 30 12 in. 2-handled oblong celery and relish tray; No. 111 10½ in. 2-handled, 5-compartment celery and relish. *Fifth row:* (left to right) No. 1 1-light hurricane lamp candelabrum with prisms; No. 5200 8 in. vase, also made in 7. in and 10 in. sizes; No. 505 10 in. footed vase, also made in 8 and 12 in. sizes; No. 507 10 in. footed vase, also made in 6, 8, and 12 in. sizes; No. 506 10 in. footed vase, also made in 8 and 12 in. sizes; No. 506 9 in. footed bud vase.

GEORGIAN*

First row: (left to right) 9 oz. goblet; 6 oz. footed ice cream or saucer champagne; 5 oz. footed ice cream; 5 oz. Jell-O; parfait; wine. *Second row:* (left to right) 12 oz. iced tea; 9 oz. table tumbler; 5 oz. orange juice; 2 oz. whiskey; grapefruit; 5 in. nappy. *Third row:* (left to right) oval Berry sugar; oval Berry cream; 6 in. ice bucket and handle, ½ gal. jug. *Fourth row:* (left to right) finger bowl and plate; teacup and saucer; 8 in. crimped vase; 8 in. No. 2-shape vase. *Fifth row:* 14 in. chop plate; 9½ in. plate; 8½ in. plate; 7½ in. plate; 6 in. plate.

---

*See color photo section.

GRECIAN

URNS, VASES, AND BOWLS

No. 550 10 in. square footed, swan-handled urn. Swan's head made as handle; also made in 8 in. crystal, ruby with crystal handles and base.

No. 545 8 in. square footed, square-handled urn. Ruby vase made with crystal handles; also available in amber, all crystal, or smoke; also made with a single handle curled upward.

First row: (top to bottom) No. 527 5½ in. square-footed vase; No. 555 6 in. square-footed comport, height—4½ in.; No. 548 10 in. square-footed vase. *Second row:* (top and bottom) No. 529 7 in. square-footed vase; No. 533 9½ in. square-footed vase. *Third row:* (top and bottom) No. 538 3½ in. square-footed cigarette holder; No. 556 8½ in. square-footed bowl, height—6 in.

HOBNAIL *

No. 118 Pattern

First row: (left to right) 9 oz. goblet; 5 oz. saucer champagne; 3½ oz. cocktail; 3 oz. wine; 10 oz. table tumbler; 13 oz. iced tea; 5 oz. orange juice. *Second row:* (left to right) 5 oz. footed Jell-O; teacup and saucer; finger bowl and 5½ in. finger bowl plate; small pepper and salt with glass top; 3½ in. cigarette jar and cover; 3 in. ashtray. *Third row:* (left to right) 3 pc. individual sugar and cream set: 5 oz. sugar, 5 oz. cream, 8 oz. oval tray; low mint box and cover; (foreground) 3 in. coaster; 7 in. handled candy basket, also made in 5 in. size; 6 oz. oil and stopper. *Fourth row:* (left to right) 12 oz. decanter and stopper; 2 oz. whiskey; 8 oz. cologne and stopper; 4 in. puff box and cover; 6 in. regular, handled nappy, also made in 5 in. size; 6 in. handled, heart-shaped bonbon, also made in 5 in. size. *Fifth row:* (left to right) 6 in. handled dessert nappy, also made in 5 and 7 in. sizes; 6 in. dessert nappy, also made in 5 and 7 in. sizes; 6 in. handled, 2-compartment relish.

---

*See color photo section.

First row: (top to bottom) 12 in. oval bowl; 10 in. square fruit bowl; 12 in. shallow salad bowl; 10 in. 2-handled crimped bowl; 10 in. 2-handled oval fruit bowl. *Second row:* (top to bottom) 4 in. candelabra with prisms; 4 in. candlestick; 9 in. 2-handled nappy; 10 in. 2-handled diamond-shaped nappy. *Third row:* (top to bottom) 12 in. crimped centerpiece; 11½ in. flared centerpiece; 11 in. 2-handled cheese and cracker set; 9 in. deep salad bowl; 12 in. crimped, oval bowl.

First row: (left to right) 8 in. low comport; 6½ in. low comport; 6 in. tall flared comport; 6 in. tall crimped comport. *Second row:* (left and right) 10 in. 2-handled, 3-compartment relish; 12 in. oval-handled basket, also made in 10 in. square shape. *Third row:* (left to right) 8½ in. salad plate; 7½ in. dessert plate; 6 in. bread and butter plate. *Fourth row:* (left to right) 11 in. 2-handled sandwich plate; 13 in. plate with flat edge, also made with rolled edge.

First row: (top to bottom) 4½ in. oval vase; 4 in. crimped vase; 6 in. top hat, also made in 10 in. size; 12 in. flip vase, also made with flared shape. *Second row:* (top to bottom) 3½ in. top hat; 5 in. footed violet vase; 5 in. footed ivy ball; 8 in. flip vase, also made with flared shape. *Third row:* (top to bottom) 2½ in. top hat; 4 in. footed ivy ball; 4 in. footed violet vase; 8 in. crimped flip vase. *Fourth row:* (top to bottom) 5 in. tall oval-handled basket; 1½ gal. flip jug; ½ lb. footed candy jar and cover, also made in 1 lb. size.

First row: (top to bottom) 6 in. footed and handled, diamond-shaped bonbon; 6½ in. footed tray; 6 in. footed and handled oval olive. *Second row:* (top to bottom) 6 in. footed and handled, flared comport; 12 in. 2-handled oval celery and relish; 3 pc. mayonnaise set: 5 in. 2-handled flared mayonnaise, 6 in. mayonnaise plate with ring, ladle. *Third row:* (top to bottom) 6 in. footed and handled oval basket; 6 in. footed and handled, crimped sweetmeat; jam jar and cover, 6 in. plate with ring.

LAGUNA*

No. 154 Pattern

Clockwise: (from top right) No. 154/49 32 oz. decanter; No. 154/34 9 in. hurricane shade and candlestick; No. 154/11 8 in. single-handled 3 pc. mayonnaise set; No. 154/35 6 in. cigarette box and handled cover; No. 154/52 12 in. hurricane shade and candlestick; No. 154/50 1-light candlestick, height—4 in. (Colors: smoky avocado, teakwood brown, or Biscayne green)

---

*See color photo section.

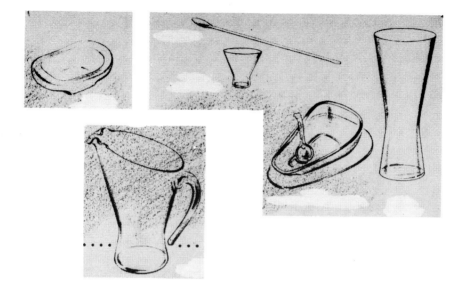

Clockwise: (from left) No. 154/36 5 in. ashtray; glass stirrer; No. 154/E 3½ oz. cocktail; No. 154/51 12 in. vase; No. 154/4 8 in. 3 pc. mayonnaise set; No. 154/33 handled ice-lip jug.

Clockwise: (from top left) No. 154/44 salt; No. 154/45 pepper; No. 154/46 oil or vinegar cruet; No. 154/48 6½ in. candy box and cover; No. 154/42 7 oz. sugar; No. 154/43 7 oz. cream.

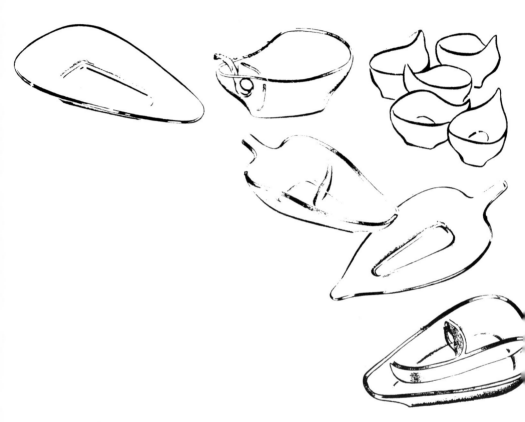

Clockwise: (from left) No. 154/29 17 in. oblong plate; No. 154/31 12 in. salad bowl with dressing compartment and ladle; 7 pc. salad service (large bowl is 12 in. x 9½ in. x 4⅝ in.; individuals are 6¼ in. x 5¼ in. x 3½ in.; salad bowl doubles as centerpiece, and individuals also serve as bonbon or nut dishes, or desserts); No. 154/32 15 in. single-handled plate; No. 154/28 14 in. 3-compartment relish; No. 154/30 14 in. single-handled, 2-compartment relish.

Laguna

After the Second World War, the taste in the American market changed to a more modern pace, and it was in 1953 that this pattern was given the Museum of Modern Art's Award for Good Design.

Plates, relish sets, cocktail glasses, beverage sets, as well as vases and hurricane lamps, were made in avocado, Biscayne green (a very dark, rich color) and brown. A simple, almost classical design, Laguna was handblown. The glasses were unusual, being quite slender at the base and wide at the top. These were designed so that one could easily grasp the article with one hand.

LANGUAGE OF FLOWERS

ETCHING IN THE KATE GREENAWAY TRADITION

First row: (left to right) 1 oz. cordial, height—4½ in.; 3 oz. wine, height
—5¾ in.; 3½ oz. liquor cocktail, height—4½ in. *Second row:* (left to right)
5 oz. footed orange juice, height—5½ in.; 5 oz. footed ice cream, height—
6¾ in.; 6 oz. saucer champagne or tall sherbet, height—4¾ in. *Third row:*
(left to right) 10 oz. goblet, height—7½ in.; 10 oz. low luncheon goblet,
height—6¾ in.; 13 oz. footed iced tea, height—7½ in. (Items described are
from No. 5331 Pattern)

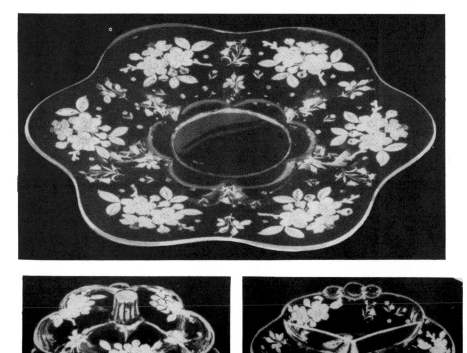

First row: (left and right) No. 30 2-light candlestick, height—6 in., width —7 in.; No. 115 3 in. low candlestick. *Second row:* (center) No. 115 14 in. plate. *Third row:* (left and right) No. 115 8 in. 3-handled, 3-compartment candy box and cover, height—4 in.; No. 115 9 in. 3-handled, 3-compartment relish, height—1½ in.

Mardi Gras

The vase in the center is from Mardi Gras, No. 42 Pattern. This vase has the following inscription on the bottom: Compliments of the *Leader*, Washington, Pa. The *Leader* was a newspaper located in Pittsburgh during the early part of 1900.

It is possible that these vases were made as an advertising item for the newspaper, as the vases were a stock item without the inscription. Some were trimmed in gold at the top.

Mardi Gras was also called Empire in an earlier catalog. They made goblets, salt and pepper shakers, salt dip, water pitchers, and a footed cake salver in this pattern. The cake salver was made with either a crystal or cobalt blue base and measured 9½ in. tall.

MURANO[*]

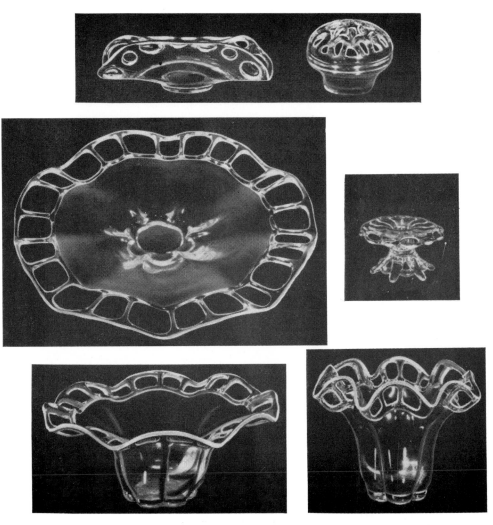

VASES AND BOWLS

First row: (left and right) No. 127 8 in. oval flower arranger, height—2½ in., width—3½ in.; No. 125 5 in. crown flower holder. *Second row:* (left and right) No. 127 14 in. plate; No. 125 2½ in. candle flower arranger. *Third row:* (left and right) No. 127 10 in. crimped bowl, height —5 in.; No. 127 7 in. flared vase.

---

[*]See color photo section.

Pall Mall*

No. 30 Pattern

First row: (left and right) 10 in. swan-handled, oval bowl, height—2¾ in., width—6¼ in.; 6 in. swan-handled, oval bowl, height—2 in., width— 3¾ in. *Second row:* (center) 11 in. swan-handled, oval bowl, height—3¼ in., width—7 in. *Third row:* (left and right) No. 30½ 12½ in. flared flower bowl, height—3½ in.; 11 in. round gardenia bowl, height—2 in. *Fourth row:* (center) 13 in. flared, crimped flower pan, height—2 in. *Fifth row:* (left and right) 12 in. crimped flower pan, height—2¾ in.; 12 in. round flower pan, height—2¾ in.

---

*See color photo section.

First row: (top to bottom) 7 in. oval, handled salad-dressing boat, height —2¼ in., width—4 in.; 7 in. oval bowl, height—2 in., width—3¾ in.; 7 in. oval mint tray, width—5¼ in. *Second row:* (top to bottom) No. 30½ 10½ in. salad bowl, height—4½ in.; 3 pc. oval mayonnaise set: 7 in. oval mayonnaise, 8½ in. oval plate, ladle; 13 in. oval bowl, height—3 in., width— 7 in., also made in 11 in. size; 15 in. oval plate, width—9½ in. *Third row:* (top to bottom) 7 in. oval salad-dressing boat, height—2¼ in., width— 4 in.; 7 in. oval mayonnaise, height—2 in., width—3¾ in., 8½ in. oval plate, width—5¼ in.

First row: (left to right) 4½ in. cigarette box and cover, height—2½ in., width—3¾ in.; 2 in. square cigarette lighter; 4 in. small (king size) cigarette box and cover, height—2¼ in., width—3¾ in. *Second row:* (left to right) 8 in. rectangular ashtray, height—1½ in., width—4¾ in.; 6½ in. rectangular ashtray, width—4¼ in.; 5 in. rectangular ashtray, width—3¼ in.; 3½ in. rectangular ashtray, width—2½ in. *Third row:* (left to right) 7 in. duck ashtray, width—4¾ in.; 6 in. duck cigarette box and cover, height—3¾ in., width—4 in.; 4 in. duck ashtray, width—2¾ in. *Fourth row:* (left and right) No. 30½ 4½ in. square ashtray; No. 30½ 3½ in. square ashtray. *Fifth row:* (left to right) 5½ in. Pimlico deep ashtray; 5 in. Pimlico ashtray; 3½ in. Pimlico ashtray.

First row: (left to right) sailfish, height—5 in., length—4 in.; 4 in. duck; 7 in. heron. *Second row:* (center) 13 in. bird of paradise, height—8½ in. *Third row:* (left and right) federal mirror bookend, height—6¾ in., width—4¾ in.; 7½ in. ruffled grouse, height—6½ in.

PASSION FLOWER

SILVER INTAGLIO ETCHING

First row: (left and right) No. 115 14 in. plate; No. 115 11½ in. oval bowl, height—5 in., width—8¼ in., also made in 10 in. size. *Second row:* (left to right) No. 534 9½ in. square, 2-handled urn; No. 30 12 in. devilled-egg plate; No. 5200 6 in. candy box and cover, height—5 in., also made in 8 in. size. *Third row:* (left to right) No. 30 12 in. rectangular floating garden, height—1¾ in., width—7½ in.; No. 30 2 in. square candlestick; No. 506 12 in. vase, also made in 10 in. size.

PLAZA*

No. 21 Pattern

Above: (clockwise from top left) goblet; No. 21½ footed tumbler; No. 21½ footed cocktail; 2-light candlestick; 16 in. flared bowl; 10½ in. handled plate; salt and pepper, noncorrosive tops; 8½ in. plate; 7½ in. plate; 6 in. plate; finger bowl plate; teacup and saucer; 10 in. regular bowl.

Below: (left to right) No. 21½ footed iced tea; No. 21½ footed orange juice; mustard and cover; oil; parfait; saucer champagne; cocktail; ice cream; wine; cordial; whiskey; orange juice; table tumbler; iced tea; flip pitcher.

*See color photo section.

RADIANCE

No. 113 Pattern

Clockwise: (from left) 14 in. plate; 4 pc. flower ensemble: 8 in. vase, 9 in. flower bowl, 12 in. flower bowl, 14 in. plate; 15 pc. punch set: 2½ gal. punch bowl, (12) handled punch cups, 18 in. rolled-edge punch tray, handled punch ladle.

First row: (left to right) 9 in. footed vase; 7 oz. sugar; 6 oz. cream; 8 in. plate, also made in 14 in. size. *Second row:* (left to right) teacup and saucer; 4 in. candlestick; 6 in. ashtray; punch ladle.

BLOWN ITEMS
No. 5113 Pattern

First row: (left to right) 14 oz. iced tea; 12 oz. iced tea; 10 oz. tumbler; 7 oz. old-fashioned; 5 oz. orange juice. *Second row:* (left to right) ½ gal. pitcher, ice-guard lip; 9 in. rose bowl; 6 in. rose bowl.

RIPPLE

No. 101 Pattern

First row: (left to right) 9 oz. tall goblet; 9 oz. luncheon goblet; 5 oz. parfait; 5 oz. saucer champagne; 3 oz. wine; 3 oz. cocktail. *Second row:* (left to right) 5 oz. footed ice cream, also made in 4 oz. size; 11 oz. footed iced tea, also made in 14 oz. size; 9 oz. footed tumbler, also made in 11 oz. size; 5 oz. footed orange juice; 2 oz. footed tumbler; 5 oz. footed Jell-O. *Third row:* (left to right) No. 100 12 oz. iced tea; No. 100 9 oz. tumbler, also made in 8 oz. size; No. 100 5 oz. orange juice; 8 oz. hotel sugar and cover; 6 oz. hotel cream; (background) finger bowl. *Fourth row:* (left to right) honey jar and cover, 6 in. plate; 6 oz. oil; 11 in. celery tray, also made in 8 in. pickle tray; water bottle: *Fifth row:* (left to right) ice cocktail and liner; 8 in. plate, also made in 6 and 14 in. sizes; ½ gal. pitcher.

RIPPLE

A pattern well named, one can almost imagine the shimmering, graceful lines of these pieces forming a series of bands around the different items, creating the look of perpetual motion. The bands are evenly spaced almost to the halfway mark on some pieces and forming a solid band up to the top.

On the plates, the inside center is plain, having six bands encircling the outside.

Two of the more unusual pieces are the honey jar and cover with the 6 in. plate, and the ice cocktail with a separate liner.

Tumblers, goblets, and a complete line of dinnerware were made in this pattern. Finger bowls and a water bottle were also popular items.

SANIBEL

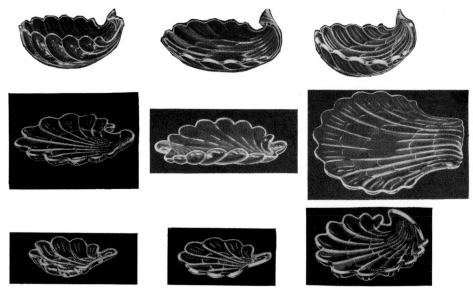

No. 130 Pattern

First row: (left to right) 11 in. deep salad bowl, height—5½ in., width—10 in.; 12½ in. shallow salad bowl, height—4¾ in., width—11¼ in.; 13 in. oval fruit bowl, height—5½ in., width—9½ in. *Second row:* (left to right) 8½ in. salad plate; 13 in. muffin tray, height—2½ in., width—7 in.; 14 in. hors d'oeuvre plate. *Third row:* (left to right) 6 in. fruit nappy, height—1¼ in.; 7 in. mint tray; 8 in. sweetmeat. (Colors: Cape Cod blue, cranberry pink, jasmine yellow, or crystal)

First row: (top to bottom) bookend vase, height—5¾ in., width—4¼ in., length—7 in.; 5½ in. footed oval vase, length—8 in., width—5 in.; 5½ in. footed, crimped vase, length—7½ in., width—4½ in. *Second row:* (top to bottom) 13 in. oblong floating garden, height—1 in., width—9¾ in.; 14 in. crimped flower bowl, height—2¾ in., width—13 in.; 14 in. floating garden, height—3 in., width—13 in.

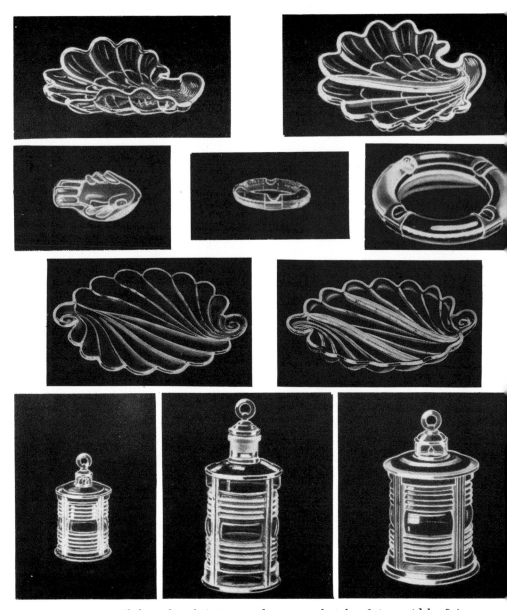

First row: (left and right) 9 in. celery tray, height—2 in., width—6 in.; 8½ in. 2-compartment relish, height—1¼ in. *Second row:* (left to right) 3½ in. tropical-fish ashtray; 3 in. life-preserver ashtray; 6 in. life-preserver ashtray. *Third row:* (left and right) 13 in. oblong sandwich plate, width —9½ in.; 13 in. 3-compartment oblong celery and relish, height—1¼ in., width—9¼ in. *Fourth row:* (left to right) 5½ in. cigarette jar and cover, diameter—2¾ in.; 30 oz. decanter, height—9½ in., diameter—4¼ in.; 9 in. candy jar and cover, diameter—4¾ in.

Sculptured Glass

ALL-SATIN FINISH

No. 128 Pattern
Sculptured Glass

This glass is called the Sculptured Pattern because it really is sculptured. These original and beautiful designs are cut painstakingly by hand by artists working in plaster. Only in this way have they been able to hold in glass a fineness of detail that is new to American glassmaking . . . the delicate detail of dogwood blossoms, the rippling curves of chrysanthemum buds, the fluttering fins of tropical fish. It is produced in crystal with raised, satin-finished figures.

SPIRAL FLUTES

Number 40 Pattern was quite popular, as it was made in a complete line of dinnerware and came in crystal, green, amber, or pink. The following items could be purchased: dinner plate; salad plate; cup and saucer; luncheon plate; nappy; handled soup; tumblers; sherbets; goblets; candlestick; finger bowls; cream and sugar; platter; and a covered vegetable dish. This particular pattern was very thin and delicate in appearance with a plain center in the plate and a rim of swirl flowing at an angle to the edge. On the drinking ware, as well as the handled soup bowls, the swirls did not go up to the edge, but had a plain band for easier drinking.

At first glance this might be mistaken for depression ware, but the quality of glass is excellent and has a distinct bell tone when touched.

SYLVAN*

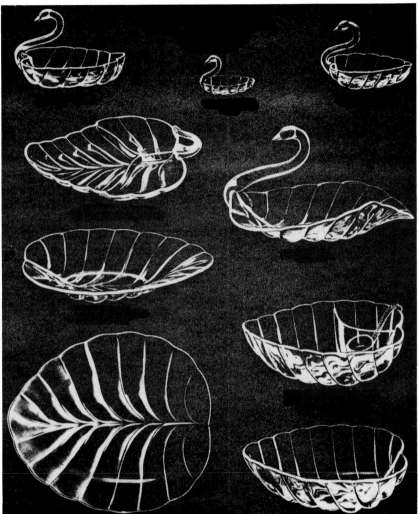

No. 122 Pattern

First row: (left to right) 7½ in. swan; 3 in. swan; 5½ swan. *Second row:* (left and right) 10 in. handled, 3-compartment celery and relish; 12 in. swan. *Third row:* (left and right) 12 in. flared flower bowl; 11 in. salad bowl with mayonnaise compartment and ladle, also for fruit and sugar or whipped cream. *Fourth row:* (left and right) 14 in. sandwich plate; 11 in. fruit bowl.

---

*See color photo section.

First row: (top to bottom) 5½ in. fruit nappy; 7½ in. candy box and cover; 7½ in. 2-compartment candy box and cover; 2 pc. canapé set: No. 501 4 oz. footed cocktail, 7½ in. handled, 2-compartment canapé plate. *Second row:* (top to bottom) 7½ in. salad plate; 7½ in. handled, 2-compartment relish; 7½ in. handled mint tray; 7½ in. 2-compartment candy dish. *Third row:* (top to bottom) 3 in. ashtray or individual nut; 5½ in. handled bonbon; 5½ in. ashtray; 7½ in. candy dish; 7½ in. 3 pc. 2-compartment mayonnaise, also available without ladles.

SYLVAN

The No. 122 Pattern adapted itself to many different uses from canapé sets to beautiful swans.

It was made in a variety of colors, crystal, and crystal with colored handles of ruby, cobalt blue, green, and amber. Many items were also made in yellow, pink, and blue opalescence. Several 7½ in. mint dishes were made in a dark green color.

On several occasions, I found a 7½ in. mint dish (minus the handle) and a 5½ in. swan to be finished on a surface resembling a close series of thousands of pencil dots.

The mint trays were also produced in milk glass with green handles. Other colored handles may have been used, but the men from the factory could not be sure. It is most likely that other colored handles may have been used because the relish trays and candy boxes were made with ruby, cobalt blue, and amber handles.

It is very difficult to state what colors were used on a particular item, as Duncan encouraged their employees to try different ideas. (Duncan had a close relationship with the workers and was highly regarded by all the people I talked to concerning this book.)

In speaking of the owners of Duncan & Miller, the employees called them by surname in almost every instance. This was one of the leading contributors to the great success that Duncan had over a period of over ninety years—the close personal relationship, the effort made by the company to encourage its men to exercise their skill and to supply both material and supplies.

No. 83 Pattern

First row: (left to right) 5 oz. parfait; No. 83½ 3 oz. cocktail; 4 in., 5 oz. ice cream; No. 83-945 5 oz. ice cream. *Second row:* (left to right) 9 oz. flared goblet; No. 83-½ 9 oz. luncheon goblet; No. 83-943 5 oz. ice cream; No. 83-941 5 oz. flared ice cream. *Third row:* (left to right) No. 83-C 11 oz. iced tea; No. 83-C 9 oz. table tumbler; No. 83-C 4 oz. grape juice; 4 in. small finger bowl; 4½ in. large finger bowl; No. 83½ 5 oz. custard or punch cup; 4½ in. nappy. *Fourth row:* (left to right) 16 oz. sugar and cover; 10 oz. cream; 6 oz. Berry sugar; 6 oz. Berry cream; 6 oz. oil and stopper. *Fifth row:* (left to right) ½ gal. pitcher; 48 oz. water bottle; qt. hotel jug; 5½ in. plate.

TAVERN

Many baskets were designed in this pattern, which was first produced in the early part of the century. It was a popular pattern due to the simplicity of design and low cost of items. Stemware and tumblers were produced, as well as many articles of tableware.

Six closely set bands circle the item about a third from its top, while 12 upright lines finish the design and end at the beginning of the circular bands because of the shape of basket, but the tumblers, sugars, creams, and other items are evenly circled.

The baskets have 24 points on the bottom and the word "PATD" stamped in the glass. At one time Duncan applied the handles separately but in later years perfected a process by which the handle and basket were one piece.

TEARDROP *

LEAD BLOWN STEMWARE
No. 5301 Pattern

First row: (left to right) 9 oz. goblet; 5 oz. saucer champagne; 4 oz. claret; 3½ oz. liquor cocktail. *Second row:* (left to right) 1¾ oz. sherry; finger bowl; 1 oz. cordial. *Third row:* (left to right) 8 oz. ale goblet; 3 oz. wine; 5 oz. ice cream; 9 oz. luncheon goblet.

---

*See color photo section.

First row: (left to right) 9 oz. footed tumbler; 8 oz. footed split or party glass; 4½ oz. orange juice; 3 oz. footed whiskey or cocktail; 2 oz. footed whiskey. *Second row:* (left and right) 5 oz. footed sherbet; 3½ oz. oyster cocktail. *Third row:* (left to right) 14 oz. footed iced tea or highball; ½ gal. pitcher with ice-guard lip; 12 oz. footed iced tea or highball.

No. 301 Pattern

First row: (top to bottom) 7 in. handled, 2-compartment relish; 5 in. handled nappy; 7 in. handled nappy; 9½ in. handled nappy; 11 in. handled plate. *Second row:* (top and bottom) 7 in. handled preserve; 8 in. handled plate. *Third row:* (top to bottom) sugar; cream; 7 in. handled, 2-compartment preserve; 7 in. 2-compartment candy box and cover; candy box and cover; 6 in. handled plate.

Clockwise: (from top left) 4 pc. lazy Susan ensemble: 18 in. plate, 12 in.
6 compartment relish, salad-dressing bowl, turntable, also made in 14 in.
size; chromium turntable used for lazy Susans; 8 in. handled, 3-compart-
ment relish; 4 pc. buffet supper ensemble: 14 in. plate, 10 in. 6-compart-
ment relish, salad-dressing bowl, also made in 18 in. size; 15 pc. punch
set: 2½ gal. punch bowl, (12) handled punch cups, 18 in. rolled-edge
punch tray, handled punch ladle; 6½ in. handled sweetmeat.

First row: 3 pc. 2-light candelabra set: 12 in. oval bowl, 2-light cande-labra. *Second row:* (left to right) 3 in. salt and pepper with glass top; (foreground) 11 in. 2 pc. cheese and cracker set; 5 in. salt and pepper with glass top. *Third row:* (left to right) 7 in. nappy; 6 in. nappy; 5 in. nappy.

First row: 3 pc. 2-light console set: 12 in. oval bowl, 2-light candlesticks. *Second row:* (left and right) 11 in. handled, 3-compartment relish; 11 in. handled celery. *Third row:* (left to right) demitasse cup and saucer; tea-cup and saucer; 3 in. individual ashtray; (foreground) 5 in. ashtray.

First row: (top to bottom) bar bottle and stopper; 4 in. candlestick; 9 in. fan-shaped vase. *Second row:* (top to bottom) 6 in. 2-compartment mint; 2 pc. 11 in. salad set: 11 in. handled plate with ring, 2-compartment mayonnaise; 12 in. oval flower bowl; 9 in. regular vase. *Third row:* (top to bottom) 6 in. low-footed comport; 6 in. ice bucket; 4 in. candlestick; 9 in. urn and cover.

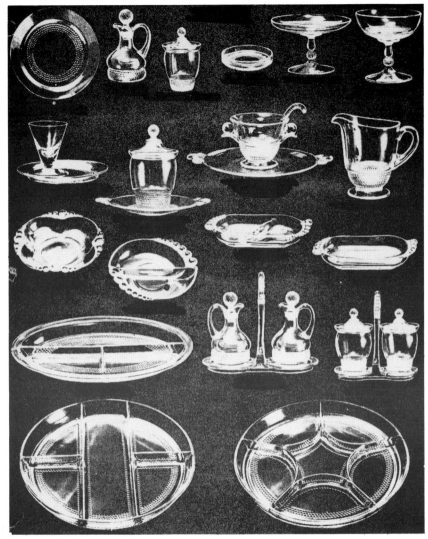

First row: (left to right) 6 in. canapé plate without ring; 3 oz. oil and stopper; mustard and cover; 3 in. coaster or ashtray; cheese stand; mayonnaise. *Second row:* (left to right) 6 in. canapé plate with ring, 3 oz. footed cocktail; 3 pc. marmalade set: marmalade and cover, 6 in. handled marmalade plate; 3 pc. mayonnaise set: 8 in. handled plate, mayonnaise, ladle; pt. pitcher, stuck handle. *Third row:* (left to right) 6 in. 4-handled bonbon; 6 in. handled, 2-compartment nut dish; 6 in. handled, 2-compartment olive; 6 in. handled pickle. *Fourth row:* (left to right) 12 in. oval 3-compartment relish; 3 pc. oil and vinegar set; 3 pc. mustard and catsup set. *Fifth row:* (left and right) No. 301½ 12 in. 5-compartment relish, also made in 10 in. size; 12 in. 6-compartment relish, also made in 10 in. size.

First row: (left to right) 4 in. candlestick; 12 in. round flower bowl; 4 in. candlestick. *Second row:* (left and right) 10 in. flared fruit bowl; 18 in. torte plate with rolled edge, also made in 13 and 14 in. sizes. *Third row:* (left) 2 pc. salad set: 9 in. salad bowl, 13 in. plate with rolled edge, also made with flat edge. *Fourth row:* (left to right) 6 in. plate; 7½ in. plate; 8½ in. plate; 10½ in. plate. 14 in. plate, also made in 18 in. size.

TEARDROP

The No. 301 Pattern is the best known of all Duncan & Miller's tableware, made in almost every conceivable piece, such as bowls, torte plates, compotes, lazy Susans, vases, and the like. Most homes have at least one piece of Teardrop in their home today.

The flawless beauty, simple but graceful lines, with rows of graduated small hobs lends itself to any table for any occasion. It could be used alone or combined with ruby or different colors. Teardrop blends particularly well when set with china. Since Teardrop was made in salad bowls, candleholders and compartment dishes, it was the most natural pattern to choose from Duncan's great variety.

The lazy Susan is featured here with a chromium turntable. It was made to fit a wooden base.

The cream and sugar had two different handles. One was made with solid handles, while the other had open-hobbed handles. The open handle was probably designed because it was much more comfortable to hold.

The salt and pepper shakers were made in 3 in. and 5 in. sizes, with glass and metal tops. The metal tops were not made at the Duncan factory, but were bought from another source, as was the turntable for the lazy Susan.

The tableware was No. 301 Pattern, the lead blown crystal No. 5301 Pattern, the tumblers No. 5300 Pattern.

TERRACE*

No. 111 Pattern

Top: 11 in. 2-handled cheese and cracker set. *Center:* (left) 9 in. salad bowl, also made in 12 in. size; (right) 10 in. flared fruit bowl. *Bottom:* 18 in. torte plate, available with rolled or flat edge, 2-compartment mayonnaise or salad-dressing bowl, mayonnaise ladles.

---

*See color photo section.

THREE FEATHERS

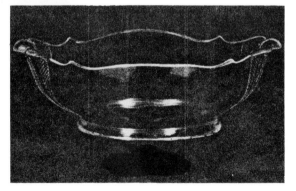

VASES AND BOWLS
No. 117 Pattern

Left to right: 7 in. 3-compartment candy box and cover, height—5½ in.; 4 in. candleholder; 12 in. oval bowl, height—4 in., width—7½ in. (The 3-compartment dish was also etched in First Love. Some of the dishes had a sterling silver base made by the International Silver Company and were used as relish dishes. The little candleholders were used as vases.)

VENETIAN

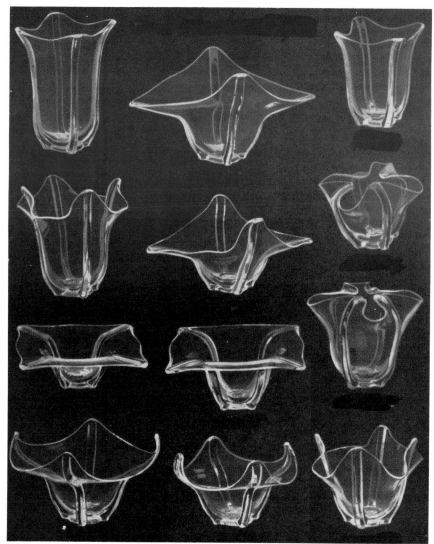

VASES AND BOWLS
No. 126 Pattern

First row: (left to right) 9 in. regular vase; 14 in. oval bowl; 7 in. regular vase. *Second row:* (left to right) 8 in. crimped, regular vase; 12 in. oval bowl; 5 in. flower holder vase. *Third row:* (left to right) 8 in. square bowl; 10 in. square bowl; 6 in. flower holder vase. *Fourth row:* (left to right) 9 in. round bowl; 8 in. round bowl; 7 in. crimped, regular vase.

VICTORIAN

First row: (left to right) 9 oz. goblet; 5 oz. saucer champagne; 4 oz. ice cream; 5 oz. parfait; 2½ oz. cocktail or wine; finger bowl and plate. *Second row:* (left to right) mayonnaise; 5 in. nappy; 8 oz. sugar; 6 oz. cream; 13 oz. highball; 7 oz. old-fashioned. *Third row:* (left to right) 12 oz. footed iced tea; 9 oz. footed tumbler; 5 oz. footed orange juice; 2 oz. footed tumbler; 7½ in. plate, also made in 6 in. size.

WATERFORD

No. 102 Pattern

First row: (left to right) 9 oz. goblet; 5 oz. parfait; 6 oz. saucer champagne; 6 oz. ice cream; 3 oz. cocktail or wine; finger bowl; ½ gal. jug. *Second row:* (left to right) 14 oz. iced tea; 12 oz. iced tea; 9 oz. table tumbler; 7½ oz. highball; 5 oz. orange juice; 2 oz. tumbler; 8½ in. plate, also made in 6 in. size.

WHITE MILK GLASS *

Betsy Ross Pattern

Above: (left to right) No. 709-14 7 in. candlestick; No. 709-6 bowl, diameter—9½ in.; No. 709-14 7 in. candlestick.

Below: (left to right) No. 709-8 5 oz. sugar and cover; No. 709-10 7 oz. sugar and cover; No. 709-7 5 oz. cream; No. 709-9 7 oz. cream.

*See color photo section.

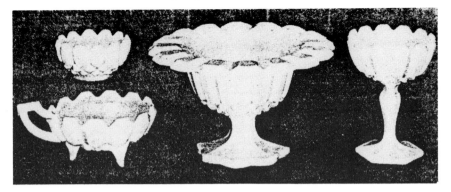

Left to right: No. 709-15 nappy, diameter—4 in.; (foreground) No. 709-13 3-toed, handled nappy, diameter—5½ in.; No. 709-11 compote, diameter—9½ in.; No. 709-17 compote, height—6 in.

Left to right: No. 709-2 8 oz. tumbler; No. 709-3 12 oz. tumbler; No. 709-1 52 oz. jug.

Left to right: No. 709-5 7½ in. 3-toed bowl; No. 709-12 footed candy box and cover; No. 709-4 urn.

Grape Pattern

Left to right: No. 719-8 7 oz. cream; No. 719-12 ½ lb. round butter and cover; No. 719-9 7 oz. sugar and cover.

Left and right: No. 719-11 vase, height—6 in.; No. 719-10 ivy bowl.

Left to right: No. 719-13 pickle, diameter—7½ in.; No. 719-7 8 oz. tumbler; No. 719-6 52 oz. jug; No. 719-5 handled olive, diameter—4½ in.

Left to right: No. 719-4 nappy, diameter—4½ in.; No. 719-3 nappy, diameter—5½ in.; No. 719-2 nappy, diameter—6½ in.; No. 719-1 nappy, diameter—7½ in.

Hobnail Pattern

Left to right: No. 718-25 4½ in. candlestick; No. 718-27 crimped bowl, diameter—11½ in.; No. 718-25 4½ in. candlestick.

Left and right: No. 718-13 13 oz. tumbler; No. 718-12 ½ gal. jug.

Left to right: No. 718-16 5 in. footed ivy bowl; No. 718-18 4 in. crimped, footed compote; No. 718-19 4 in. flared, footed compote.

Left to right: No. 718-11 2-compartment relish, diameter—6 in.; No. 718-10 nappy, diameter—6½ in.; No. 718-9 nappy, diameter—7 in.

Left and right: No. 718-5 deep, flared nappy, diameter—8 in.; No. 718-6 9 in. 2-handled salad bowl.

Clockwise: (from left) No. 718-28 crimped vase, height—8 in.; No. 718-8 10 in. footed cake salver; No. 718-4 deep, regular nappy, diameter—8 in.; No. 718-21 3½ in. jam jar and cover; No. 718-23 5 oz. cream; No. 718-24 5 oz. sugar.

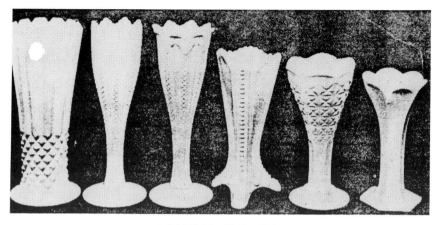

ACCESSORY ITEMS

Left to right: No. 709-16 vase, height—10 in.; No. 742-2 regular vase, height—8 in.; No. 742-1 flared vase, height—8 in.; No. 750-1 tripanel vase, height—9 in.; No. 708-83 vase, height—9 in.; No. 754-1 vase, height—7½ in.

Left to right: No. 763-5 vase, height—6 in.; No. 708-61 handled urn; No. 708-27 lily bowl; No. 708-31 handled compote, height—6 in.

Left to right: No. 708-21 scalloped-edge nappy, diameter—8 in.; No. 708-4 rose bowl, height—7½ in.; No. 708-104 candy box and cover.

Left to right: No. 712-3 6 in. square wedding bowl and cover, height—
12 in.; No. 712-2 5 in. square wedding bowl and cover, height—10 in.;
No. 712-1 4 in. square cigarette box and cover, height—6½ in.

Clockwise: (from left) No. 786-1 vase, height—6 in.; No. 763-21 wall
vase; No. 730-1 duck ashtray, length—7 in.; No. 771-1 vase, height—6½
in.; No. 730-2 duck candy box and cover.

Counterclockwise: No. 763-4 handled nappy, diameter—5 in.; No. 763-3
nappy, diameter—4½ in.; No. 763-1 footed compote, height—8½ in.; No.
763-2 bowl, diameter—9 in.

SPECIAL PIECES OF DUNCAN

Cracker Jar. This cracker jar was said to be chosen by J. Ernest Miller to be the pattern for his first set of dinnerware. It is very similar to the No. 331 line and has an early American appearance. This item is quite heavy in both weight and design. It has a block within a large square outstanding with deep, indented lines going from top to bottom. The bottom is ground flat around a star-shaped pattern which has elongated points. The glass has very high brilliance. The knob on the top of the lid has an all-over block.

The *No. 153 Candlelight Garden Set* had a 2 in. candlestick that fit inside
the 6½ in. ashtray to make an unusual flower arranger, or to be used as
a 3 pc. set with the ashtray in the center and a candlestick on either side.
These were made in crystal, light blue, dark green, ruby, and blue
opalescent.

Donkey, Cart, and Peon. The 3 pc. set consisted of a donkey, cart, and peon. This was one of Duncan & Miller's most popular sets. It is very difficult to find a set with all pieces in perfect shape, as the handles of the cart seemed to break very easily. Most of these sets were made in crystal, but a few were frosted. Some of the original molds were sold in the United States, and a few were said to have been bought in Mexico. The reproductions were frosted, but one can identify the Duncan & Miller figures easily. Scratch the bottom of the figure lightly—it will be clear under the frosting.

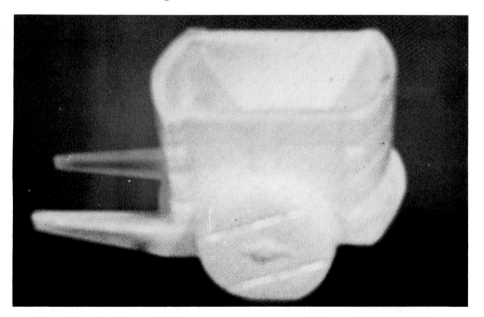

Cart. The Opalescent White piece is very rare. The cart has the appearance of being milk glass and is part of the 3 pc. set of the donkey, peon, and the cart.

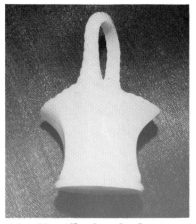

This lovely little *No. 61 milk glass basket* is approximately 5 in. in height, about 2 in. wide at the base, and is 4½ in. wide at the top of the basket. It has a fluted edging going up and around the handle and has vertical ridges going from the opening down almost to the bottom, where it has a smooth base with a star-cut bottom. The basket curves in very slightly where it joins the base. This had a pressed handle.

These were made in crystal too, which were sold either plain, cut, or etched. Made in many sizes, some ranged up to 13 inches or more. The price for a dozen crystal baskets this size was $1.70.

Octagonal Plate. This eight-sided plate was made in crystal, green, pink and amber. Salad plates and small, round candy dishes can be found in this pattern. It is believed to have been made by Duncan & Miller as a special order for another company. It is an all-over design with an outside, deep rim of swirls and leaves with a five-pointed star showing many times throughout the plate. The edge is pointed but not rough. The underside is ground and polished.

Hurricane Lamp. The No. 1 1-light hurricane lamp with prisms has a No. 505 chimney. The chimney is decorated in various patterns, such as, First Love, Adoration, and Passion Flower, as illustrated.

Swans were made in many different shapes and sizes. The most well known is Pall Mall, the No. 30 Pattern. The following sizes and colors were available: 3½ in. crystal, light blue, green, avocado, teakwood, ruby, and amber; 7 in. crystal, light blue, green, avocado, ruby, teakwood, pink, and blue opalescent; 10½ to 12 in. crystal, light blue, green, avocado, teakwood, ruby, and amber, and possibly in the opalescent, but I have not been able to verify this.

The 3½ in. crystal swan once sold for $1.50, while the ruby color was listed at $2.00 for that size. One of the catalogs listed a fifth size, which was 6 inches. It was the same shape as the 7 in. but was deeper, and this made the difference in length. It was not listed on the old price sheets I have, so it is assumed it was not a stock item. These facts may help to clear up the confusion many people have had concerning the two sizes.

The open swans with designs cut on them were also not a regular production line but were finished that way for friends or for the company's own use.

Many of these had flowers, shafts of wheat, combinations of swirls and lines. These are very beautiful and are highly prized by their owners today.

The swans having gold and sterling silver designs on the bodies were shipped to other companies to be decorated and were very popular for wedding and anniversary gifts.

Three Face. The No. 400 celery was designed by J. Ernest Miller. One early piece he made was a cake plate, which was awarded a prize at the Centennial Exposition in Philadelphia in 1876. He had designed this particular plate in the winter of the previous year and decided to display this unusual item. The stem showed two profiles, and yet the full face would be clearly visible. Other items made by Mr. Miller following his award were received with enthusiasm and were as follows: goblets, clarets, champagnes, celery dishes, cake plates or salvers in 9, 10, and 11 in. sizes, water pitchers, creamers, biscuit jars, comports made open or with lid in 7, 8, 9, and 10 in. sizes, lamps, and salts made open and also with metal top. Some had a frosted base and face, but a few were clear. When the Duncan plant in Pittsburgh was destroyed by fire in 1892, the molds were supposedly lost to collectors forever, but the story did not end. Due to popular demand, the large comport (with or without the cover) was produced again by using a sandcast mold from a Three-Face comport. This was done at a brake shoe company located in Rochester, New York. The mold was assembled at the Washington Mold Company in Washington, Pennsylvania, at the end of the forties. A feeling of great pride must be felt by all the men and women who played even a minute part in the reconstruction of that particular item and also to the remaining members of the families of the late Mr. Miller and his lovely bride. In a price catalog in the early fifties, the Three-face comport was listed at $20 or $30 with a lid. These items came under Duncan special pieces and were the only two pieces listed at that time.

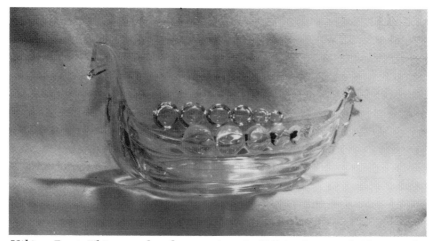

Viking Boat. This very handsome piece is 11½ in. long and 6½ in. wide. It is an open-glass article with the front shaped like the prow of a Viking ship. On the sides, in the center, are 6 round, graduated circles of glass that overhang the outside of the boat. The Vikings used these as shields and would hang their weapons on them while they were sailing. Four divided bands of glass encircle the ship down to the base. As were most pieces of Duncan & Miller, this was ground on the bottom and made in crystal.

SPECIAL SETS AND MISCELLANEOUS ITEMS

Ashtrays and Smokers Sets

First row: (counterclockwise) No. 13 4 in. ashtray; No. 14 3½ in. ashtray; No. 15 3 in. ashtray; No. 18 3½ in. ashtray; No. 16 5 in. ashtray; No. 12 3 in. oval cigarette holder: No. 101 3½ in. ashtray, book or box of matches; No. 1 3 in. coaster or ashtray. *Second row:* (left to right) No. 12 5 in. club ashtray; No. 11 4 in. ashtray; No. 10 2½ in. ashtray; No. 17 4½ in. ashtray. *Third row:* (left to right) No. 301 3 in. individual ashtray; No. 301 5 in. ashtray; No. 18 4½ in. cigarette box and cover; No. 100 3½ in. small cigarette box and cover. *Fourth row:* (left and right) No. 100 6 pc. princess cigarette set: 4½ in. cigarette box and cover, 3 in. cigarette ashtrays; No. 50 6 pc. hostess cigarette set: cigarette jar and cover, 3 in. cigarette ashtrays.

MISCELLANEOUS DRINKING AND SMOKING ITEMS

First row: (left to right) No. 55 32 oz. decanter and stopper; No. 55 16 oz. decanter and stopper; No. 46 8 oz. bitter bottle and tube; No. 46 2 oz. bitter bottle and tube; No. 56 16 oz. decanter and stopper; No. 56 32 oz. decanter and stopper. *Second row:* (left to right) No. 55 12 oz. highball; No. 55 9 oz. tumbler; No. 55 6 oz. split; No. 55 4 oz. orange juice; No. 55 1½ oz. whiskey; No. 46 1½ oz. whiskey; No. 45 1¼ oz. whiskey. *Third row:* (left and right) No. 116 6 pc. smoking set: cigarette box and cover, individual ashtrays; No. 901 Tom and Jerry or punch set: 1½ gal. punch bowl, punch cups, No. 30 18 in. rolled-edge punch tray, ladle. *Fourth row:* (left to right) No. 46 7 oz. old-fashioned; (background) No. 46 5 oz. old-fashioned; No. 11 30 oz. cocktail shaker with chromium top; No. 11 16 oz. cocktail shaker with chromium top; No. 11 16 oz. martini mixer with chromium cap and spoon; No. 11 30 oz. martini mixer with chromium cap and spoon; No. 46 muddler.

BAR AND BEVERAGE SETS

Gordon decanter No. 55 came in crystal with a crystal or ruby stopper. It was also made in frosted glass, a satin finish with clear, blue, or ruby stoppers.

The No. 56 decanter was made in both crystal or frost with clear or colored stoppers. The glasses were frosted to match the decanters.

The No. 55 bar line, was made in crystal, cobalt blue, and ruby. From the corners of the points of the square base there was a straight edge extending almost to the top of the glass, giving the effect of three dimensions. Inside the square base was a circle. The glass curved in very slightly toward the top. Made in five different sizes, these were popular in the thirties.

Decanters were also available to match the designs for the owl, fish, rooster, sea horse, and Waikiki tumblers. Wine glasses were also sold to match these particular items.

Beverage sets included tumblers, ice cocktails with cocktail inserts, sherbets, juices, and ice tubs.

FOOTED TUMBLERS
Colored Foot with Novelty Cuttings

First row: (left to right) No. 500 14 oz. footed highball, cut—owl; No. 500 12 oz. footed highball, cut—fish; No. 500 9 oz. footed tumbler, cut—rooster; No. 500 8 oz. footed highball, cut—Waikiki; No. 500 7 oz. footed old-fashioned, cut—rooster; No. 500 5 oz. footed orange juice. *Second row:* (counterclockwise) No. 500 3½ oz. footed orange juice; No. 500 2 oz. footed whiskey; No. 500 footed martini mixer with chromium cap and spoon, cut—fish; No. 500 30 oz. footed cocktail shaker with chromium top, cut—sea horse; No. 501 3 oz. cocktail, cut—fish; No. 501 4 oz. cocktail, cut—sea horse; No. 9 8 in. coupe plate, cut—sailfish; No. 8 6 in. canapé plate, cut—fish, No. 501 cocktail, cut—fish. *Third row:* (left to right) No. 502 14 oz. footed highball, cut—sea horse; No. 502 12 oz. footed highball, cut—sailfish; No. 502 10 oz. footed highball, cut—sea horse; No. 502 8 oz. footed highball, cut—fish; No. 502 7 oz. footed old-fashioned, cut—owl; No. 502 5 oz. footed orange juice; No. 502 2 oz. footed whiskey. (Colored foot available in green, amber, royal blue, sapphire blue, ruby, or all crystal; also available with any cutting shown or plain)

BOWLS

First row: (top to bottom) No. 8 12 in. flared bowl; No. 16 12 in. oval bowl; No. 41 12 in. oblong bowl; No. 117 12 in. oval flower bowl; No. 115 12 in. round flower bowl. *Second row:* (top to bottom) No. 14 12 in. oval bowl; No. 75 11 in. crimped bowl; No. 301 12 in. round flower bowl. *Third row:* (top to bottom) No. 111 10 in. regular, footed bowl; No. 112 12 in. round flower bowl; No. 113 12 in. round flower bowl; No. 301 12 in. oval bowl; No. 115 12 in. oval bowl.

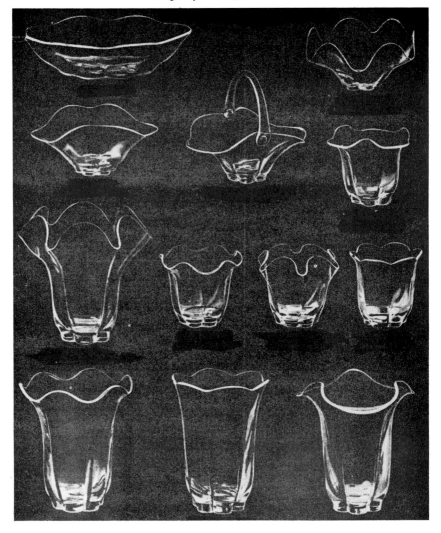

FLOWER BOWLS AND VASES

First row: (left and right) No. 115 13 in. flared oval bowl; No. 115 9 in. crimped bowl, also made in 10½ in. size. *Second row:* (left to right) No. 115 10 in. oval bowl, also made in 11½ in. size; No. 115 10 in. oval handled basket, also made in 11½ in. size; No. 115 5 in. cloverleaf vase, also made in 6½ in. size. *Third row:* (left to right) No. 115 10½ in. flower arranger, also made in 8½ in. size; No. 115 5½ in. crimped vase, also made in 7 in. size; No. 115 5½ in. flower arranger, also made in 7 in. size; No. 115 6 in. vase, also made in 7 in. size. *Fourth row:* (left to right) No. 115 10 in. crimped vase, also made in 8 in. size; No. 115 12 in. vase, also made in 9 in. size; No. 115 10 in. cloverleaf vase, also made in 8½ in. size.

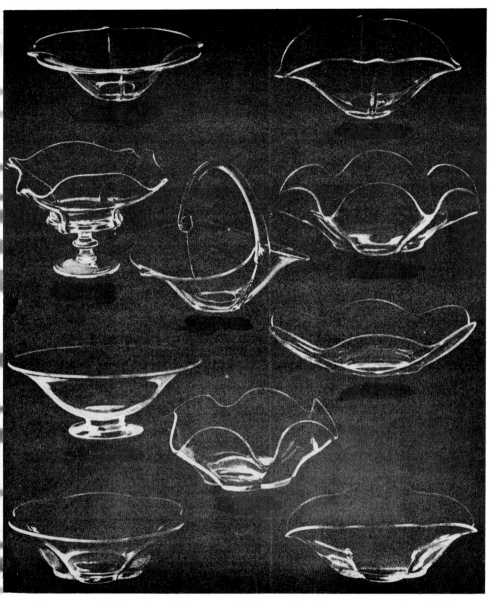

First row: (left and right) No. 126 12 in. flared centerpiece; No. 126½ 12 in. oval bowl. *Second row:* (left to right) No. 126 10 in. square, footed bowl; No. 126 12 in. oval handled basket; No. 115 13 in. crimped, oval bowl. *Third row:* (left to right) No. 30 13 in. flared, low-footed bowl; No. 115 12 in. crimped salad bowl; No. 115 15 in. shallow salad bowl. *Fourth row:* (left and right) No. 115 12 in. flared bowl; No. 115 13 in. oval bowl.

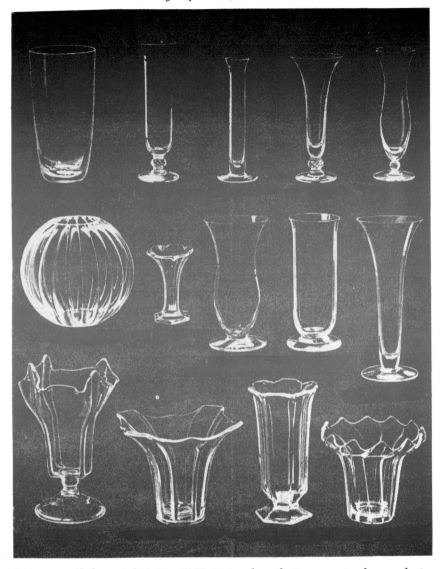

First row: (left to right) No. 5200 10 in. sham-bottom vase, also made in 7 and 8 in. sizes; No. 509 9 in. vase; No. 506 9 in. bud vase; No. 510 9 in. bud vase; No. 508 9 in. vase. *Second row:* No. 5113 9 in. rose bowl, also made in 6 in. size; No. 120 6 in. footed vase; No. 505 10 in. footed vase, also made in 8 and 12 in. sizes; No. 506 10 in. footed vase, also made in 8 and 12 in. sizes; No. 507 12 in. footed vase, also made in 6, 8, and 10 in. sizes. *Third row:* (left to right) No. 126 12 in. crimped, footed vase; No. 119 8½ in. flared vase; No. 120 10 in. footed vase, also made in 5½, 12, and 14 in. sizes; No. 121 7 in. flared, cupped vase.

Display Sign. These were given to the different jewelry and department stores that sold the glassware. The round circle is 5 in. by 5 in., and the total height is about 6 in.

A *badge* worn by the workers at the Duncan & Miller plant.

Astaire. This pattern was listed in two different catalogs under different names, but with the same pattern number. Kimberly was ruby decorated, and Hilton was decorated in colony blue. It is believed the different names were used to identify the different colors. Color was fused for permanence and was a great favorite as it was sold at a very modest price and blended well with casual, everyday living. It was designed for Early American decor. The combination of a cross mark at the center of a glass or item, combined with a close series of very small impressions at the bottom and the smooth wide rim at the top, made this a perfect balance for setting a lovely table. The set shown is *Hilton*, a very rare 5 pc. dresser set consisting of puff box, 2 perfume bottles, powder box and tray. The glass tray has the original Duncan sticker. It was crystal with cobalt covers and stoppers. The tray is cobalt blue.

Chanticleer. This very popular line of barware was made in crystal, ruby, cobalt blue, and amber. The green and blue colors were available in a frosted effect. Cocktail shakers and old-fashioned glasses were made in this pattern. The 7 oz. old-fashioned glasses shown are blue and green, while the 3½ oz. cocktail glass is clear. The martini mixers were available in two sizes—16 and 32 oz. It is called "Barnyard" by many people because of the farm scene.

No. 500 Cocktail Shaker and Glasses: 30 oz. cocktail shaker; 14 oz. highball; 9 oz. tumbler; 5 oz. juice. Available in crystal with a ruby, amber, royal blue, or green foot.

No. 52 Crown Punch Bowl. The original composition consisted of 12 5 oz. punch cups, a punch ladle, a 21 in. tray, and an 8 qt. 13 in. punch bowl. This was also made in a 15 in. flared, 7 qt. bowl.

No. 112 Caribbean Punch Bowl Set. 15 pc. punch set (see section on punch bowls).

No. 103 Georgian Wine Glass. This pattern was a favorite with restaurants because of the design and because it could be obtained in a wide range of colors: crystal, ruby, green, amber, blue, and pink. Colored handles of ruby, green, cobalt blue, and amber were applied to some of the 9 oz. water tumblers and sold as mugs, which are prize collectors items today. The Georgian tumblers are curved in at the top and do not stack evenly. This was done on purpose and helps to identify them. They were supposed to set in one row with a flat divider, such as a large restaurant tray placed on top of the row of glasses. They are not ground on the bottom, as are so many of Duncan's ware.

Hobnail. Made in many different tablepieces, stemware, baskets, bowls, and hats, this was one of Duncan & Miller's best-selling patterns. This was one of the company's earlier lines and was produced in crystal, blue, pink, amber, red, rose, and opalescent blue. The amber and rose are rarely seen today. All sandwich trays, bowls, nappys, and plates are ground on the bottom. Each tiny hobnail seems to reflect thousands of sparkling diamonds shining in the sunlight. Most of the items, such as trays, had five rows of hobs, graduating from small to larger ones from a single round hob in the center of the bottom of the article. The ground bottom started from the last outside row of hobs. From the base of the bowl or tray the hobs began to graduate again for approximately nine rows, then became a little more uniform to the top and edge of the item with outside round ones. I say approximately nine rows because it would depend on the size of the piece; that is, a small creamer in Hobnail only has nine rows in the bowl and two on the base edge. It does not always have a ground edge on the base, which may be due to several reasons. For instance, the piece may not have been suited for grinding. The baskets and cream pitchers would have been very difficult to grind as the hobs extended to the edge of the item and completed the design of that particular piece. Another reason was, in identifying the item which you may have, that particular one may have been a second that was not ground. The workers were permitted to buy these seconds at a very low cost, which accounts for some of the wares not being ground on the bottom.

The Duncan & Miller Company was very thorough with the finished product. Great pride on the part of these workers is responsible for the beautiful ware that is so eagerly sought after today. They were great craftsmen who took pleasure in doing their job and doing it well.

Some of the pieces that did not have hobs to the top but were finished by a smooth band were as follows: 4½ in. oval vase; 3½ in. top hat; 2½ in. top hat; 6 in. top hat; 5 in. handled basket; 5 in. footed violet vase with ruffled top; 4 in. footed violet vase with ruffled top; 4 in. ivy ball; 5 in. ivy ball; 1½ gal. jug; 12 in. flip vase; 8 in. flip vase with smooth edge and ruffled; footed candy jar and cover, with hobs covering the knob of lid; goblets; saucer champagnes; cocktails; wine tumblers; iced teas; juice glasses; Jell-O; and teacup and saucer. The oil and vinegar had the design about halfway to the center of bottle.

6 in. Hobnail top hat.

No. 118 Pink Opalescent Hobnail. (Background) 13 in. round plate; (center) 12 in. oval bowl; (right and left) 4 in. candlesticks, also made in blue opalescent and crystal.

Crystal Wine Cup with Ruby Applied Handles. The base is solid, clear glass, and nine rows of hobs encircle the cup almost to the top. The bottom is smooth.

No. 154 Laguna Salt Shaker.

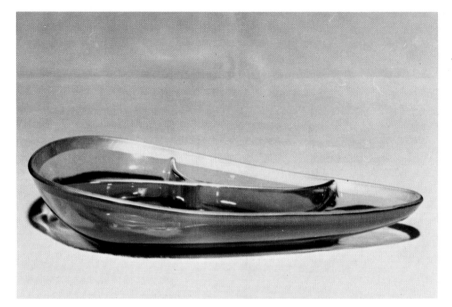

No. 154 Laguna 3-Compartment Relish Dish. 14 in. long and trimmed in gold, most of this pattern was not trimmed. Made in teakwood and smokey avocado.

No. 30 Pall Mall Cigarette Box and Ashtrays. These were cut in a design that brought out the maximum brilliance of Duncan & Miller glass. This blank was also used when etching First Love, Adoration, and the Mallard Duck. The box measures 4½ in. high and 3½ in. wide. The ashtrays are 5 in. by 3¼ in. and complete the set, along with the smaller ones (3½ in. sq.). These were very popular items and used in many different designs.

No. 30 Pall Mall Frosted Swordfish. This was made in crystal, frosted (pictured above), and blue opalescent. This one is ground flat and clear on bottom.

Heron. Also made in crystal. These were used in the center of shallow bowls to create a most unusual centerpiece.

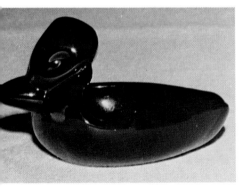

Black Duck Ashtray. Extremely rare, this was not a regular line but was probably made as a favor to one of the employees. The standard colors were crystal, ruby, and light blue.

No. 30 Pall Mall Ruffled Grouse. Very rare, these pieces weigh approximately 5 lbs. The grouse is 6½ in. high and 7½ in. long. They were very difficult to make, and because of the outstretched tail, these pieces had a very high rate of breakage. Some were frosted on the tail and the collar for outstanding effects.

Water Pitcher with Swan-Neck Handle. This one has the Mallard Duck design etched on the bottom half of the pitcher. It was called Silver Intaglio etching and was used on cigarette boxes, ice buckets, and decanters. The pitcher is crystal, with the wildlife scene emphasized in a frosted effect. This design was a great favorite and popular in the forties.

This extremely rare *ruby solid swan* was not a production line, but made for one of the men as a special piece, as was the *milk glass swan*.

No. 30 *Pall Mall Swans* show the regular line of solid swans made by Duncan in three sizes: 3 in., 5 in., and 7 in.

Ruby Swan. Available in 3½ in., 7 in., 10½ in., and 12 in. sizes. The colors are crystal, green, avocado, teakwood, and pink and blue opalescent.

No. 122 5½ in. Sylvan Swan (left) and *No. 118 5 in. Blue Opalescent Hobnail Basket* (right), available in clear or pink opalescent.

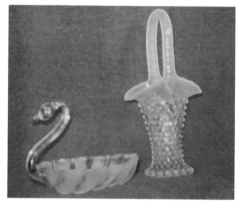

No. 122 Sylvan Swan (left), (center) *No. 130 13 in. 3-Compartment Relish,* (right) *No. 130 8½ in. Salad Plate.*

Swan given away by Duncan & Miller for souvenirs. Inside the bottom of the base of the swan is the inscription "Genuine Duncan."

No. 3 Vase. This lovely cobalt blue vase is 9 in. tall and 6½ in. wide and has a three-sided effect. The full front view of the swan is shown with outspread wings, as if in flight; the head is tucked down to complete the effect. This was made in crystal and green also.

10½ in. Milk Glass Swan with Green Neck. This rare piece was also made with ruby or cobalt blue necks and could be bought in the 7 in. size. It is ground on the bottom.

No. 122 Sylvan Swan. This 12 in. swan is in blue opalescent. It is also available in a 3 in. size. The 5½ in. size is 5 in. tall and 5¼ in. wide; the 7½ in. size is 5½ in. tall and 6½ in. wide. The 12 in. swan is 10½ in. in height and 11¾ in. wide and is available in clear and pink opalescent.

7 in. Amber Swan with Solid Amber Neck; 3½ in. swan with clear neck and amber body; 7 in. swan with candleholder in the center. This was also made in ruby.

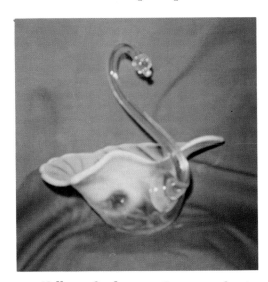

Yellow Opalescent Swan made in crystal, amber, green, and blue. This was called W and F and may also be found in frosted colors of amber and pink.

No. 21 Plaza Salt Shaker. Also made in pink and crystal.

No. 301 Teardrop Cream and Sugar. A warm, chocolate color instead of crystal, these pieces were made as an experiment for one of the institutes. The glass is quite heavy in contrast to the regular weight of Teardrop.

Milk Glass. These three items in the milk glass are extremely rare. The basket (left) is 11½ in. tall with a clear, soft green applied handle 9¾ in. lengthwise and approximately 5 in. in width where the handles are placed. These figures vary a little because each person pinched in a bit differently. The design is No. 115 Canterbury. The next item is No. 122 Sylvan 2-compartment relish (right) with green handle, 1 in. in height and 6½ in. by 7½ in. The bonbon dish (foreground) and handle are all milk glass, 1¾ in. high and 5½ in. wide by 5½ in. in length. Duncan & Miller made these handles in green, ruby, and cobalt blue.

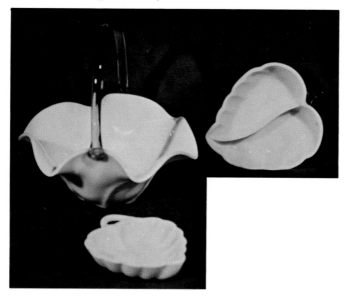

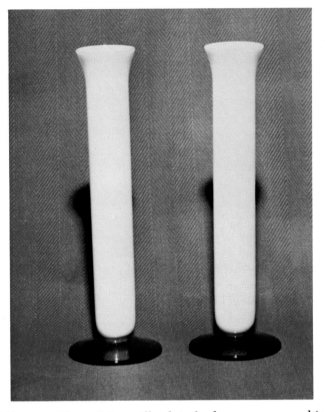

No. 506 Pattern. These 9 in. milk glass bud vases are combined with ruby bases to create a stunning effect. Other colors used on the base were cobalt blue and green. Some of the same materials that were used in making milk glass were needed by our government during the Second World War. As a result, Duncan & Miller Glass Company discontinued making milk glass and also opalescent, cranberry, pink, and sapphire blue to insure the Defense of Freedom Program the support needed for our country during those critical years.

No. 555 Shell and Tassel, Square and Round. Augustus H. Heisey did the patent design for the square shell and tassel pattern in the year 1881. He was a very versatile man, holding the office of secretary for the company of George A. Duncan & Sons at that time. He was one of the partners in the original company formed by his father-in-law, George Duncan, Sr., having married Susan Duncan. He had been a colonel in the Union Army during the Civil War. He decided to go his own direction and formed the A. H. Heisey Glass Company in 1895.

Shell and tassel have a very rough, pebbly finish with interlacing lines. On the bowls and cake plate the edge is scalloped, except in the center where a flat line is formed and it is smooth to the touch. A cord

or tassel hangs down into a point. The base of the bowl has a star cut in the center; on the outside is a scalloped cording with tiny dots in the center of the cord and a tiny, diamond-shaped point that stands out between each scallop. The bowl is 9¾ in. long and 5½ in. wide. There are 13 scallops on each side from the center of the bowl. The tray is 13½ in. long and 9 in. wide in the center. The tray *does not* indent in the sides, but the side tassels come almost to the cording in the bottom of the tray. The sides of the tray are frosted, and there is an extra frosted line going through each dot. This glass comes in different colors (crystal, amber), and it was reported to have been made in blue. It has a brittle finish and will chip quite easily. Also made in this pattern were cake stands, compotes, and 7½ in. shell comports.

Duncan & Miller encouraged their employees to create new designs, and as a result the lovely cut vase on page 122 was supposedly inspired by an "off-hand worker." It was his job to see that different ideas were presented. One such design was this beautiful *vase* standing approximately 13 in. high. It has 9 slender bands of cobalt blue glass spiraling around the top of the vase. Six rows of glass bands complete the base. The top of the vase is cut with flowers and leaves. The color is a very soft blue.

Terrace. Duncan & Miller had always had the reputation of producing the unusual, so when the No. 111 Pattern was introduced, its modern design was met with approval by those who were looking for a futuristic design. The colors were ruby, cobalt blue, crystal, and amber. The square dinner plate could be used as a service plate for other plates, such as green Sandwich, to create an unusual table arrangement. First Love and Adoration were etched on many of these blanks, creating a striking product. The stemware had three rows of straight lines on the stem and the cup handle has a winged effect. Some of the pieces were decorated in gold, as was the lovely covered candy dish shown.

Sugar Shaker. Made for the Pittsburgh Restaurant Supply Co. The tops were not made at the Duncan plant and were mscribed on the lid with "Pittsburgh Restaurant Company."

No. 28 3-Pc. Hospital Tray Set. 5 oz. sugar; 4 oz. cream; 3 in. butter, which made the set complete. This blank was also used for etching with First Love and Adoration.

This lovely cruet was made by Richard Dimmack of Washington, Pennsylvania, while working as a mold maker in the Duncan & Miller plant; this cruet was one of a kind. The men were encouraged to try new ideas, and as a result the workers would use their creative ability to produce many such items. The relationship between the workers and the owner was very close. This is today one of the facts that is responsible for the great interest in Duncan & Miller glassware in Washington, Pennsylvania, and all over the United States. The true test of the success of a person or a company depends on whether the feats they have accomplished are remembered, and, most of all, if the people care enough about the past to make it a part of the future. I believe this was true when the workers produced their one-of-a-kind pieces.

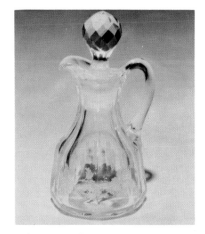

Vinegar Cruet with Amber Stopper.

No. 54 Crystal Cruet. Leaf design cut around base; pressed stopper.

Covered 3-Compartment Candy Dish (left). No. 115 blank made in crystal, blue, amber, pink and blue opalescent, and ruby. This was also etched with First Love, Passion Flower, Indian Tree. (Center) *Cornucopia.* Colors are the same as candy dish. The tail is sometimes curled up or swirled in a downward motion. (Right) *Horn of Plenty.* Made in clear, blue, pink and yellow opalescent, and etched with First Love, Indian Tree, Passion Flower, or Language of Flowers.

Ruby Candleholder. Also available in amber and crystal with crystal handle.

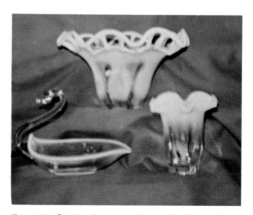

7 in. Pink Opalescent Swan (left), and *No. 127 Murano Crimped Bowl* (center), 10 in.

No. 129 Puff Box. This was part of a 3-pc. perfume set which was made in crystal and also in frosted and crystal. The covered box measures 5¾ in. high and was large enough to be used as a candy dish. A 7 in. perfume bottle completes the set. The stoppers are almost half the height of the bottle. It was almost spillproof, as the weight of the bottles were designed to balance the height of the stoppers.

Serving Tray or Bed Tray. These glass inserts are decorated in pink or blue flowers with a faintly colored background, and are designed to slide between the metal bars. It is 9½ in. long and 10½ in. wide and has plastic handles.

No. 41 Sandwich Syrup Jug. 13 oz. capacity.

No. 28 9 oz. Tumbler. The foot was made in ruby, green, cobalt blue, amber, rose, and ebony. The top of the glass was crystal. Between the top part of the glass and the base of the glass was a band of solid glass. The foot was applied separately.

6-Compartment Relish Dish. Made with frosted animals on No. 301 blank, this is 12 in. wide.

Testing mold of the donkey which was part of a 3-pc. set that consisted of a peon, donkey, and cart. These were used to make sure the molds were correct in every detail. This one is made of lead and is now used as a doorstop. The base was not on the original glass donkey.

Another testing mold is of the little *glass centennial hatchet;* inscribed on the top half of the hatchet is 1810 October 2-2 1910. The handle says Washington, Pennsylvania. Duncan made other glass hatchets that were larger, measuring 6¼ in. in length and were 3½ in. wide. These were plain and did not have any lettering on them. The hatchets were made in crystal.

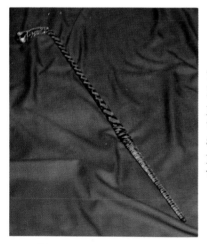

The *glass canes* were carried in the Labor Day Parade, and the men who participated were permitted to keep them. Some were very elaborate with swirls of color twisted in the upper part next to the handle. The parades were well attended by the men.

One of the *ribbons* worn in parade and also at funerals—Associated Flint Glass Worker Union #55. These were beautiful ribbons, with the two clasped hands at the top of the ribbon and the two crossed American Flags. On the left side of the hands it says, "United we stand," and on the right side, "Divided we fall." These ribbons were a source of great pride to the men at Duncan & Miller Glass Company.

Bowls

Candleholders were available to match the No. 16 Pattern bowl. This particular pattern made in crystal, rose, and green. There were a few made in ebony (jet black).

The Three Feathers, No. 117 Pattern, bowl used the tiny cornucopias for candleholders.

The Caribbean, No. 112 Pattern, candleholders were quite tall and were made in crystal and blue.

Ice buckets were quite popular and were sold in crystal, pink, and green.

Other items made in ebony were a crimped bonbon, a cigarette box, ashtrays, and a bonbon dish. Duncan made many other pieces in this color, including the No. 16 Pattern bowl.

No. 16 12 in. flared oval bowl with matching candlesticks. This console set was made in pink crystal, green, and black. The candlesticks are 6 in. tall. I have also seen this set with a etched design of flowers.

Cut glass bowl (left), width—12 in.; twin mayonnaise bowl (right). Both are on the No. 115 blank, Canterbury.

CANDELABRA

First row: (left to right) No. 14 1-light candelabrum with U prisms, height—8 in.; No. 14 2-light candelabrum with U prisms, height—7½ in., width—8 in.; No. 14 3-light candelabrum with U prisms, height—8 in., width—10 in. *Second row:* (left to right) No. 21 2-light candelabrum with U prisms, height—6 in., width—9 in.; No. 111 1-light candelabrum with C prisms, height—9 in.; No. 111 2-light candelabrum with C prisms, height—7 in., width—9½ in. *Third row:* No. 112 1-light candelabrum, height—8 in.; No. 112 2-light candelabrum, height—6 in., width—8 in., stubby prisms; No. 301 2-light candelabrum, height—6 in., width—8½ in., stubby prisms; No. 115 1-light candelabrum with U prisms, height—7 in. (Candelabra available without bobeches and prisms for use as candle-sticks)

Clockwise: (from left) No. 1-C 3-light candelabrum with U prisms, height—16 in., width—13 in., 3 bobeches; No. 1 1-light candelabrum with U prisms, height—10 in.; No. 1 epergne with U prisms, height—12 in., width—13 in., No. 1-B 3-light candelabrum with U prisms, height—10 in., width—13 in., 2 bobeches.

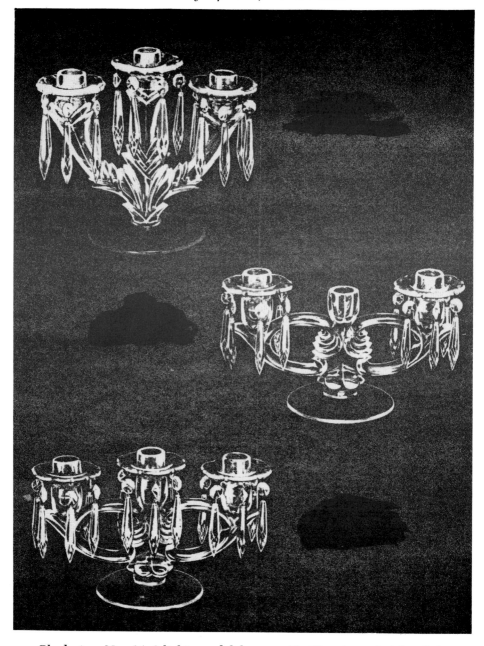

Clockwise: No. 14 3-light candelabrum with U prisms, height—8 in., width—10 in.; No. 115 3-light candelabrum with U prisms, height—7 in., width—11 in., 2 bobeches; No. 115 3-light candelabrum with U prisms, height—7 in., width—11 in., 3 bobeches.

Clockwise: (from left) No. 1 3-light candelabrum with U prisms, height —24 in., width—18 in.; No. 1 1-light candelabrum with U prisms, height —10 in.; No. 1 5-light candelabrum with U prisms, height—24 in., width —18 in.; No. 65 1-light candelabrum with U prisms, height—11½ in.

CANDELABRA

Most of Duncan's candelabra could be interchanged to fit other candlesticks; that is, the bobeches and prisms could be used to create an entirely different effect. The prisms were imported from other countries and were not made in the factory.

MISCELLANEOUS ITEMS*

First row: (left to right) No. 26 5 oz. mustard and cover; No. 26 3½ in. coaster; No. 31 3 in. coaster; No. 26 3 in. nappy. *Second row:* (left to right) No. 106 6 in. 3-compartment candy box and cover; No. 25 11 in. cheese and cracker set, 11 in. cheese plate with ring, No. 934 cheese stand; (background) No. 35 5½ in. nappy, also made in 4½ and 6½ in. sizes; No. 31 6 in. low-footed comport. *Third row:* (left to right) No. 33 9 in. nappy, also made in 8 in. size; No. 31½ 10 in. 5-compartment relish, also made in 12 in. size; (background) No. 35 9 in. nappy, also made in 8 in. size; No. 31 10 in. water tray, also made in 12 in. size. *Fourth row:* (left and right) No. 31 10 in. 6-compartment relish, also made in 12 in. size; No. 26 10½ in. handled lunch plate.

---

*Miscellaneous items include the following: baked-apple dish, candy dish, cheese and cracker set, celery, compartment relish dish, console set, grapefruit, hospital tray set, ice cream sherbet, ice tub, mustard jar, nappy, oyster cocktail, and vase.

First row: (left to right) No. 908 5 oz. sugar; No. 908 5 oz. cream; No. 908 demitasse cup and saucer; No. 908 teacup and saucer. *Second row:* (left to right) No. 908 bouillon cup and saucer; No. 908 cream soup and plate; No. 908 finger bowl and plate. *Third row:* (left to right) No. 29 5 in. nappy, also made in 5½ in. size; No. 29 6 in. grapefruit, also made in 6½ in. size; No. 30 7½ in. baked apple; No. 30 9 in. oyster plate. *Fourth row:* (left to right) No. 30 8½ in. star-bottom plate, also made in 6 and 7½ in. sizes; No. 30 7½ in. plate, also made in 6, 8½, 10½, 12, 14, and 18 in. sizes; No. 30 6 in. low-footed comport.

First row: (left to right) No. 61 2½ oz. oyster cocktail; No. 61-C 9 oz. tumbler; No. 65 2¾ in. salted almond. *Second row:* (left to right) No. 61 4 oz. oil and stopper, also made in 2 and 6 oz. sizes; No. 61 4 oz. handled custard; No. 61 2 oz. individual cream; No. 61 3 oz. individual sugar. *Third row:* (left to right) No. 61 14 oz. sugar; No. 61 11 oz. cream; No. 61 8 oz. hotel sugar and cover; No. 61 5 oz. hotel cream. *Fourth row:* (left to right) No. 61 8 in. pickle tray; No. 65 6½ in. spoon tray; No. 65 8 in. pickle tray; (foreground) No. 65 10 in. celery tray. *Fifth row:* No. 61 48 oz. water bottle; No. 65 4 oz. footed sherbet; No. 61 11 in. celery tray.

First row: (left to right) No. 28 6 in. candlestick; No. 28 4 in. candlestick; No. 50 6 oz. sugar; No. 50 5½ oz. cream. *Second row:* (left to right) No. 91 4½ in. nappy; No. 91 5½ in. nappy; No. 55 12 oz. handled mug. *Third row:* (left and right) No. 91 11 in. celery tray; No. 91 8½ in. pickle tray. *Fourth row:* No. 50 3 pc. console set: 12 in. oval bowl, 3 in. candlesticks. *Fifth row:* (left to right) No. 12 9 in. vase; No. 28 7 in. ice bucket and handle; No. 28 6 in. ice bucket and handle.

First row: (left to right) No. 28 12 oz. footed, optic iced tea; (background) No. 28 9 oz. footed, optic tumbler; No. 28 4 oz. footed, optic orange juice; (background) No. 28 5 oz. footed, optic ice cream; No. 28 3½ oz. footed, optic sherbet; (background) No. 27 3 in. coaster; No. 1 3 in. coaster. *Second row:* (left to right) No. 101 ice cocktail set: 11 oz. ice cocktail goblet, 3 oz. ice cocktail liner; No. 25 footed grapefruit, 5 oz. footed grapefruit liner; No. 25 5 oz. peg-footed grapefruit liner; No. 219 2½ oz. oyster-cocktail center; No. 220 3 oz. oyster-cocktail center; No. 218 4 oz. cocktail center. *Third row:* (left to right) No. 25 5 in. handled nappy, also made in 6 in. size; No. 25 5 in. nappy, also made in 3½, 4, 4½, 5, 5½, and 6 in. sizes; No. 25 5 in. ice cream nappy, also made in 6 in. size; No. 57 6½ in. grapefruit. *Fourth row:* (left to right) No. 30 7 in. ice tub; No. 25 9 in. nappy, also made in 7 and 8 in. sizes; No. 28 6 in. muffin cover; No. 28 3 pc. hospital tray set: 5 oz. hospital sugar, 4 oz. hospital cream, 3 in. hospital butter.

Punch Bowl Sets

Name	Pattern Number
Bristol Diamond	44
Caribbean*	112
Crown*	52
Hobnail	118½
Homestead	63
Mardi Gras	42
Plaza	65
Radiance	113½
Teardrop	301
Venetian	126
————	901

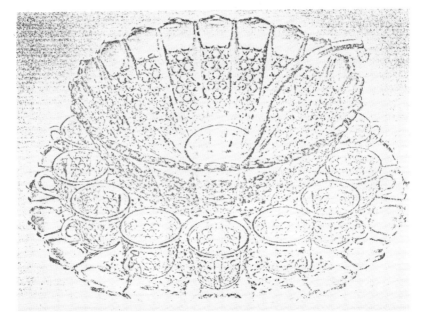

No. 44 Bristol Diamond. 15 pc. punch set: 8½ qt., height—15½ in., or 9 qt., height—13½ in. flared punch bowl; (12) punch cups; 21 in. tray; ladle. This pattern is one of Duncan's loveliest, and it is a rare delight to find a complete set.

---

*See color photo section.

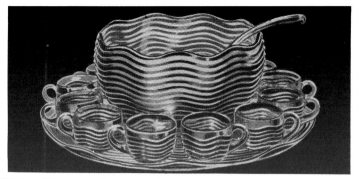

*No. 112 Caribbean** 15 pc. punch set: 1½ gal, punch bowl, height—6 in.; (12) 5 oz. punch cups, stuck handle; 18 in. tray with rolled edge; ladle; cups and ladle available with crystal, ruby, cobalt blue, or amber handles.

No. 118½ Hobnail. 15 pc. punch set: 1½ gal. punch bowl, height—5¼ in.; (12) 5 oz. punch cups, pressed handle; 16 in. tray; ladle.

No. 63 Homestead. 15 pc. punch set: 6½ qt. punch bowl, height—15 in., or 2 gal. punch bowl, height—12½ in.; (12) 5 oz. punch cups; 21 in. tray; ladle.

---

*See color photo section.

No. 42 Mardi Gras (originally listed as Empire). 16 pc. punch bowl set: 2 gal. punch bowl, height—14½ in., or 2½ gal. punch bowl, height—13 in.; (12) 5 oz. punch cups; 21 in. tray; ladle; 5¼ in. foot.

No. 301 Teardrop. 15 pc. punch bowl set: 2½ gal. punch bowl; (12) handled punch cups; 18 in. tray with rolled edge; ladle; 5 oz. cups also available.

No. 126 punch bowl set is different from most sets in that it does not have a tray. Made in crystal, punch cups and ladle are also available in crystal with ruby, amber, and cobalt blue handles.

No. 901 punch bowl set. 15 pc. set: 1½ gal. punch bowl; (12) 5 oz. punch cups; 18 in. tray; ladle.

No. 113½ punch bowl set. 15 pc. set: 1½ gal. punch bowl, height—6¼ in.; (12) 5 oz. punch cups, pressed handle; 18 in. tray with rolled edge; ladle.

No. 65 Plaza. 15 pc. punch bowl set: 7½ qt. punch bowl, height—15½ in., or 13½ in. punch bowl; (12) 5 oz. punch cups; 21 in. tray; ladle.

ROCK CRYSTAL CUTTINGS

Name	Pattern Number
Alhambra	607
Andover	760
Belfast	734
Berkeley	702
Chantilly	773
Chesterfield	717
Concord	701
Coronet	682
Empress	696
Eternally Yours	765
Exeter	758
Juno	688
Kohinoor	690
Killarney	686
Laurel Diamond	733
Laurel Wreath	640
Lexington	764
Lovelace (gray cut)	681
Marlborough	628
Maytime	698
Monterey	697
Minuet	713
Nobility	775
Palmetto	720
Phoebus	621
Prelude	763
Saratoga	769
Sheffield	768
Stratford	689
Sun Ray	691
Tiara	683
Tripole	750
Tristan	622

First row: (left and right) JUNO DESIGN—rock crystal cutting No. 688 on No. 5317 Cathay stemware; STRATFORD DESIGN—rock crystal cutting No. 689 on No. 504 Granada stemware. *Second row:* (left and right) KOHINOOR DESIGN—rock crystal cutting No. 690 on No. 5322 Erin stemware; SUN RAY DESIGN—rock crystal cutting No. 691 on No. 5322 Erin stemware.

First row: (left to right) VICEROY DESIGN—rock crystal cutting No. 695 on No. 5321 Trianon stemware; EMPRESS DESIGN—rock crystal cutting No. 696 on No. 5375 Diamond stemware; MONTEREY DE-SIGN—rock crystal cutting No. 697 on No. 5375 Diamond stemware. *Second row:* (left to right) CONCORD DESIGN—rock crystal cutting No. 701 on No. 5323 Alden stemware; BERKELEY DESIGN—rock crystal cutting No. 702 on No. 5322 Erin stemware; VIRGINIA DARE DESIGN—rock crystal cutting No. 703 on No. 5323 Alden stemware.

First row: (left and right) CORONET DESIGN—rock crystal cutting No. 682 on No. 5317 Cathay stemware; KILLARNEY DESIGN—rock crystal cutting No. 686 on No. 5323 Alden stemware. *Second row:* (left to right) WELLINGTON DESIGN—rock crystal cutting No. 629 on No. 34 Kent stemware; LOVELACE DESIGN—rock crystal cutting No. 681 on No. 5317 Cathay stemware (matches 1847 Rogers Bros. Lovelace silverplate; TIARA DESIGN—rock crystal cutting No. 683 on No. 5321 Trianon stemware.

First row: (left and right) TRISTAN DESIGN—rock crystal cutting No. 622 on No. 5115 Canterbury stemware; LAUREL WREATH DESIGN— rock crystal cutting No. 640 on No. 503 Touraine stemware. *Second row:* (left to right) ALHAMBRA DESIGN—rock crystal cutting No. 607 on No. 504 Granada stemware; PHOEBUS DESIGN—rock crystal cutting No. 621 on No. 5115 Canterbury stemware; MARLBOROUGH DESIGN —rock crystal cutting No. 628 on No. 34 Kent stemware.

First row: (left to right) PALMETTO DESIGN—rock crystal cutting No. 720 on No. 34 Kent stemware; NOBILITY DESIGN—rock crystal cutting No. 775 on No. 5330 Dover stemware; TRIPOLE DESIGN—rock crystal cutting No. 750 on No. 5115 Canterbury stemware. *Second row:* (left and right) BELFAST DESIGN—rock crystal cutting No. 734 on No. 5323 Alden stemware; EXETER DESIGN—rock crystal cutting No. 758 on No. 5329 Wistar stemware.

First row: (left and right) MAYTIME DESIGN—rock crystal cutting No. 698 on No. 5115 Canterbury stemware; MINUET DESIGN—rock crystal cutting No. 713 on No. 5317 Cathay stemware. *Second row:* (left and right) CHESTERFIELD DESIGN—rock crystal cutting No. 717 on No. 32 Windsor stemware; LAUREL DIAMOND DESIGN—rock crystal cutting No. 733 on No. 5322 Erin stemware.

First row: (left and right) ANDOVER DESIGN—rock crystal cutting No. 760 on No. 5329 Wistar stemware; PRELUDE DESIGN—rock crystal cutting No. 763 on No. 5331 Victory stemware. *Second row:* (left and right) ETERNALLY YOURS DESIGN—rock crystal cutting No. 765 on No. 5331 Victory stemware (matches 1847 Rogers Bros. Eternally Yours silverplate); WILSHIRE DESIGN—rock crystal cutting No. 767 on No. 5330 Dover stemware.

First row: (left and right) SHEFFIELD DESIGN—rock crystal cutting No. 768 on No. 5330 Dover stemware; CHANTILLY DESIGN—rock crystal cutting No. 773 on No. 5115 Canterbury stemware. *Second row:* (left to right) LEXINGTON DESIGN—rock crystal cutting No. 764 on No. 5331 Victory stemware; SARATOGA DESIGN—rock crystal cutting No. 769 on No. 5330 Dover stemware; VICTORY DESIGN—rock crystal cutting No. 772 on No. 5331 Victory stemware.

LEAD BLOWN STEMWARE

Name	Pattern Number
Alden	5323
Cathay	5317
Deauville	5326
Diamond	5375
Dover	5330
Erin	5322
Granada	504
Kent	34
Terrace	5111½
Touraine	503
Trianon	5321
Victory	5331
Windsor	32
Wistar	5329

If you would see one of the oldest crafts known to man, yet surviving a machine age, you should visit that department of the Duncan factory where they make delicate, glistening stemware. Yes, there have been improvements in methods, but basically the blowing of glass has not changed in a thousand years.

Watch the gatherer as he collects on the end of a blowpipe a glob of white quartz sand, soda ash, lead, lime, potash, nitrate, and borax, carefully preheated into a molten mass. Watch him as he preshapes it by carefully rolling it on a polished steel plate, and at the same time slowly blows a bubble in the glob, which gradually enlarges.

Watch the blower as he takes the blowpipe with the partially formed shape, and by perfect coordination of lung, eyes, and hands, the result of years of training, completes the shaping of it with the aid of a carefully prepared mold. When he has finished, you are amazed at the transformation into a goblet fit to toast a princess.

You are entranced. You pick it up and flick it with your finger. It rings like a bell. You begin to realize why blown glass is expensive. You even marvel how anything that requires so much skill, so many operations, could cost so relatively little.

And the blowing is not all. Your goblet must be annealed to relieve the stresses and strains that would cause it to shatter at the slightest jar. Then it may be decorated, cut, or etched. Before it is shipped it may have passed through the hands of a dozen craftsmen, each an artist in his line, imbued with a love of the beautiful and the pride of accomplishment.

We like to think of Duncan stemware, standing there in all their crystal brilliance, as symbols reflecting the past, foretelling better things to come.

As you show the shapes and patterns illustrated on the following pages, think of the history behind each one.

ALDEN

No. 5323 Pattern

First row: (left to right) 10 oz. goblet, height—6 in.; 6 oz. saucer champagne or tall sherbet, height—4¼ in.; 5 oz. claret, height—5¼ in.; 3 oz. wine, height—4¾ in. *Second row:* (left and right) 3½ oz. liquor cocktail, height —4¼ in.; 6 oz. footed ice cream, height—3 in. *Third row:* (left to right) 13 oz. footed iced tea, height—5¾ in.; 5 oz. footed orange juice, height— 4¼ in.; 4½ oz. oyster cocktail, height—3¼ in.; finger bowl, diameter—4¼ in.

CATHAY

No. 5317 Pattern

First row: (left to right) 10 oz. goblet, height—6¼ in.; 5 oz. saucer champagne, height—4½ in.; 5 oz. claret, height—5¾ in.; 3 oz. wine, height—5 in. *Second row:* (left to right) 3½ oz. liquor cocktail, height—4 in.; 1 oz. cordial, height—3½ in.; 4½ oz. oyster cocktail, height—3½ in.; 5 oz. footed ice cream, height—3½ in. *Third row:* (left to right) 12 oz. footed iced tea, height—6½ in.; 9 oz. footed tumbler, height—5½ in.; 5 oz. footed orange juice, height—4¾ in.; finger bowl, diameter—4½ in.

DEAUVILLE

No. 5326 Pattern

First row: (left to right) 9 oz. goblet, height—7¾ in.; 5 oz. saucer champagne, height—6 in.; 4½ oz. claret, height—6¾ in.; 3 oz. wine, height—6¼ in.; 3½ oz. liquor cocktail, height—5¼ in. *Second row:* (left to right) 1 oz. cordial, height—5 in.; 4½ oz. oyster cocktail, height—4¼ in.; finger bowl, diameter—4½ in. *Third row:* (left to right) 13 oz. footed iced tea, height —6¾ in.; 9 oz. luncheon goblet, height—6 in.; 5 oz. footed orange juice, height—4¾ in.; 6 oz. ice cream, height—3¾ in.

DIAMOND

No. 5375 Pattern

First row: (left to right) 9 oz. goblet, height—7¼ in.; 6 oz. saucer champagne, height—5½ in.; 5 oz. claret, height—6½ in.; 3½ oz. liquor cocktail, height—5 in.; 3 oz. wine, height—5¾ in. *Second row:* (left and right) 1 oz. cordial, height—4¼ in.; 4½ oz. oyster cocktail, height—3¾ in. *Third row:* (left to right) 6 oz. ice cream, height—3¾ in.; 12 oz. iced tea, height—6½ in.; 9 oz. footed tumbler or low goblet, height—5½ in.; 5 oz. orange juice, height—4¾ in.

DOVER

No. 5330 Pattern

First row: (left to right) 10 oz. goblet, height—5¾ in.; 6 oz. saucer champagne or tall sherbet, height—4½ in.; 5 oz. claret, height—5¼ in.; 3 oz. wine, height—4¾ in.; 3½ oz. liquor cocktail, height—4 in. *Second row:* (left to right) 1 oz. cordial, height—3½ in.; 4½ oz. oyster cocktail, height—3½ in.; finger bowl, diameter—4¼ in. *Third row:* (left to right) 13 oz. footed iced tea, height—6½ in.; 10 oz. footed tumbler, height—5⅞ in.; 5 oz. footed orange juice, height—4½ in.; 5 oz. ice cream, height—3½ in.

ERIN

No. 5322 Pattern

First row: (left to right) 9 oz. goblet, height—6 in.; 6 oz. saucer champagne or tall sherbet, height—4½ in.; 4½ oz. claret, height—5¼ in.; 3 oz. wine, height—4¾ in.; 3½ oz. cocktail, height—4¼ in. *Second row:* (left and right) 4½ oz. oyster cocktail, height—3½ in.; 6 oz. footed ice cream, height —3¼ in. *Third row:* (left to right) 13 oz. footed iced tea, height—6 in.; 5 oz. footed orange juice, height—4½ in.; finger bowl, diameter—4¼ in.

GRANADA

No. 504 Pattern

First row: (left to right) 10 oz. goblet; 5 oz. saucer champagne; 3½ oz. liquor cocktail; 5 oz. claret; 3½ oz. wine. *Second row:* (left to right) 2 oz. sherry; 1 oz. cordial; 5 oz. footed ice cream. *Third row:* (left to right) 12 oz. footed iced tea; 10 oz. footed tumbler; 5 oz. footed orange juice; 3 oz. footed whiskey; 4½ oz. oyster cocktail.

KENT

No. 34 Pattern

First row: (left to right) 10 oz. goblet, height—7¾ in.; 6 oz. saucer champagne, height—6¾ in.; 4½ oz. claret, height—6¾ in.; 3 oz. wine, height—6 in.; 4 oz. cocktail, height—6 in. *Second row:* (left to right) 1 oz. cordial, height—3¾ in.; 4 oz. oyster cocktail, height—4 in.; 12 oz. footed iced tea, height—7 in.; 6 oz. footed orange juice, height—5¼ in.; finger bowl, diameter—4½ in.

TERRACE

No. 5111½ Pattern

First row: (left to right) 10 oz. goblet, tall stem, height—6¾ in.; 5 oz. saucer champagne, tall stem, height—5 in.; 3½ oz. liquor cocktail, height —4½ in.; 4½ oz. claret, tall stem, height—6 in.; 3 oz. wine, height—5¼ in. *Second row:* (left to right) 10 oz. low luncheon goblet, height—5¾ in.; 1 oz. pousse-café, height—3¾ in.; 1 oz. cordial, height—3¾ in.; 4 oz. oyster cocktail, height—3¾ in.; finger bowl, diameter—4¼ in. *Third row:* (left to right) 14 oz. footed iced tea, height—6¾ in.; 12 oz. footed iced tea, height—6½ in.; 5 oz. footed orange juice, height—5¼ in.; 3 oz. footed whiskey, height—4½ in.; 5 oz. footed ice cream, short stem, height—4 in.

TOURAINE

No. 503 Pattern

First row: (left to right) 10 oz. goblet, height—6½ in.; 6 oz. saucer champagne, height—4¾ in.; 3½ oz. liquor cocktail, height—4½ in.; 5 oz. claret, height—5½ in.; 9 oz. goblet, height—6¾ in. *Second row:* (left to right) 2½ oz. wine, height—4¾ in.; 2 oz. sherry, height—4¾ in.; 2 oz. crème de menthe, height—4 in.; 1 oz. cordial, height—3½ in.; 5 oz. ice cream, height—3½ in.; 3½ oz. oyster cocktail, height—3¾ in. *Third row:* (left and right) finger bowl, height—2¼ in.; cigarette holder, height—3¼ in. *Fourth row:* (left to right) 2 oz. footed whiskey, height—3¼ in.; 5 oz. footed orange juice, height—4¾ in.; 9 oz. footed tumbler, height—5½ in.; 12 oz. footed iced tea, height—6½ in.; 10 oz. luncheon goblet, height—5 in.

TRIANON

No. 5321 Pattern

First row: (left to right) 10 oz. goblet, height—7½ in.; 6 oz. saucer champagne or tall sherbet, height—6 in.; 5 oz. claret, height—6¾ in.; 3 oz. wine, height—6¼ in.; 3 oz. liquor cocktail, height—5½ in. *Second row:* (left and right) 1 oz. cordial, height—4½ in.; 4½ oz. oyster cocktail, height—3½ in. *Third row:* (left to right) 3 oz. footed iced tea, height—6¼ in.; 5 oz. footed orange juice, height—4½ in.; 6 oz. footed ice cream, height—3½ in.; finger bowl, diameter—4½ in.

VICTORY

First row: (left to right) 10 oz. goblet, height—7½ in.; 6 oz. saucer champagne or tall sherbet, height—4¾ in.; 5 oz. claret, height—6 in.; 3 oz. wine, height—5¾ in.; 3½ oz. liquor cocktail, height—4½ in. *Second row:* (left to right) 2 oz. sherry, height—4¾ in.; 1 oz. cordial, height—4¼ in.; 4½ oz. oyster cocktail, height—4¾ in.; 5 oz. footed ice cream, height—6¾ in. *Third row:* (left to right) 13 oz. footed iced tea, height—7½ in.; 10 oz. footed tumbler, height—7 in.; 5 oz. footed orange juice, height—5½ in.; finger bowl, diameter—4½ in.

WINDSOR

First row: (left to right) 9 oz. goblet, height—7 in.; 5 oz. saucer champagne, height—4½ in.; 3 oz. liquor cocktail, height—4¾ in.; 4 oz. claret, height—5¾ in. *Second row:* (left and right) 3 oz. wine, height—5½ in.; 1 oz. cordial, height—3¾. *Third row:* (left to right) 12 oz. footed iced tea, height—6½ in.; 5 oz. footed orange juice, height—4¾ in.; 4 oz. oyster cocktail, height—4 in.; finger bowl, diameter—4¼ in.

WISTAR

No. 5329 Pattern

First row: (left to right) 10 oz. goblet, height—7¾ in.; 6 oz. saucer champagne or tall sherbet, height—6¼ in.; 3½ oz. liquor cocktail, height—5½ in.; 5 oz. claret, height—7 in.; 3 oz. wine, height—6½ in. *Second row:* (left to right) 1 oz. cordial, height—4¾ in.; 6 oz. footed ice cream, height—3½ in.; finger bowl, diameter—4½ in. *Third row:* (left to right) 13 oz. footed iced tea, height—6½ in.; 9 oz. footed tumbler or luncheon goblet, height—5½ in.; 5 oz. footed orange juice, height—4½ in.; 4½ oz. oyster cocktail, height—4 in.

STEMWARE DESIGNS

First row: (left to right) ATHENA DESIGN, height—5¾ in.; FERN DE-
SIGN, height—5¾ in.; GOVERNOR CLINTON DESIGN, height—5¾ in.;
RIDGEWOOD DESIGN, height—6¾ in.; ETERNALLY YOURS DE-
SIGN, height—7½ in.; FRANCIS FIRST DESIGN, height—7¾ in. *Second
row:* (left to right) CHINESE GARDEN DESIGN, height—5¾ in.;
SPRING GLORY DESIGN, height—5¾ in.; MESA DESIGN, height 6¾
in.; LILY OF THE VALLEY DESIGN, height—6¾ in.; QUEEN'S LACE
DESIGN, height—7¼ in.; NOBILITY DESIGN, height—5¾ in.

First row: (left to right) DAWN DESIGN, height—6¼ in.; CRETAN DESIGN, height—6¼ in.; BELVEDERE DESIGN, height—6¾ in.; WILD FLOWER DESIGN, height—6¾ in.; PICKWICK DESIGN, height—6¼ in.; HOLIDAY DESIGN, height—6¼ in. *Second row:* (left to right) FLEUR-DE-LIS DESIGN, height—6¼ in.; HAWTHORNE DESIGN, height—6¼ in.; WHEAT DESIGN, height—6¼ in.; SUNDOWN DESIGN, height—6¼ in.; SPRAY DESIGN, height—6¼ in.; WILD ROSE DESIGN, height—6¼ in.

STEMWARE PATTERNS

CANDLELIGHT

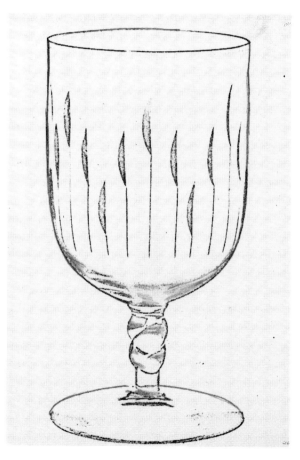

TRADITIONAL

Stemware items available: goblets, saucer champagnes or tall sherbets, liquor cocktails, wines, footed seafood cocktails, footed iced teas, footed fruit juices; height of goblet—5¼ in.; pattern includes 7½ and 8½ in. plates.

CANTERBURY

CONTEMPORARY OR EIGHTEENTH CENTURY

Stemware items available: low goblet, low sherbet, footed iced tea, footed juice or wine, footed cocktail; height of goblet—5¼ in., capacity—14 oz.; pattern includes 7½ and 8½ in. plates; flatware also available. (All stemware items are No. 5115½)

RADIANCE

TRADITIONAL AND PROVINCIAL

Stemware items available: goblets, saucer champagnes or tall sherbets, liquor cocktails, wines, cordials, footed seafood cocktails, footed iced teas, footed fruit juices; height of goblet—5¾ in.; pattern includes 7½ and 8½ in. plates.

SPRING BEAUTY

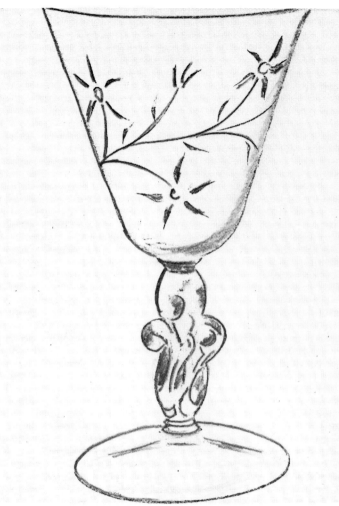

This is a rock crystal cutting on the shape number D5-1. Stemware items available: goblets, wines, saucer champagnes, tall sherbets, cordials, footed seafood cocktails, footed juices, footed iced teas, liquor cocktails; height of goblet—6¼ in.; pattern includes 7½ and 8½ in. plates. (Cretan, Dawn, and Hawthorne were also cut on the D5-1 shape.)

STARLIGHT

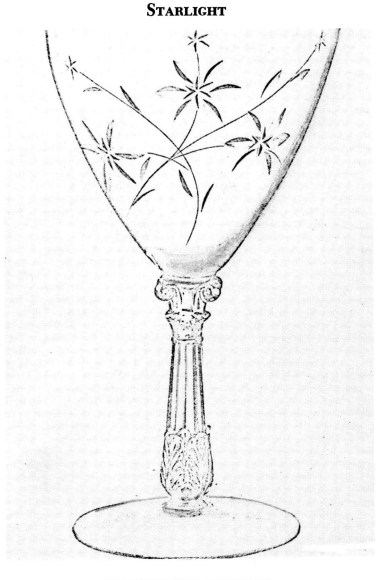

EIGHTEENTH CENTURY

Stemware items available: goblets, saucer champagnes or tall sherbets, liquor cocktails, wines, cordials, footed seafood cocktails, footed iced teas, footed fruit juices; height of goblet—7 in. (also available in low goblet, No. 5152, height—5 in., and low sherbet, No. 5152, height—3¾ in.); pattern includes 7½ and 8½ in. plates.

SUNDOWN

CONTEMPORARY AND MODERN PROVINCIAL

Stemware items available: goblets, saucer champagnes or tall sherbets, liquor cocktails, wines, footed seafood cocktails, footed iced teas, footed fruit juices; height of goblet—6¼ in.; pattern includes 7½ and 8½ in. plates.

TEARDROP

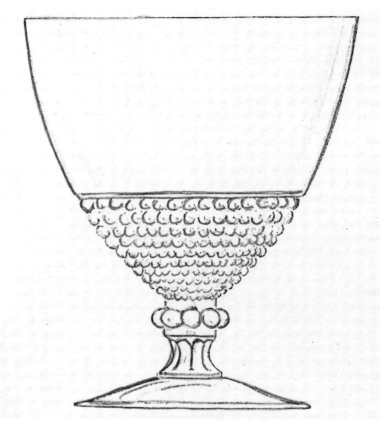

CONTEMPORARY OR EIGHTEENTH CENTURY

Stemware items available: low goblets, low sherbets, footed iced teas, footed juices or wines, footed cocktails; height of goblet—5 in., capacity —14 oz.; pattern includes 7½ and 8½ in. plates; flatware also available. (All stemware items are No. 5301½)

WILD ROSE

CLASSIC AND CONTEMPORARY

Stemware items available: goblets, saucer champagnes or tall sherbets, liquor cocktails, wines, cordials, footed seafood cocktails, footed iced teas, footed fruit juices; height of goblet—6¼ in.; pattern includes 7½ and 8½ in. plates.

WILLOW

TRADITIONAL AND PROVINCIAL

Stemware items available: goblets, saucer champagnes or tall sherbets, liquor cocktails, wines, cordials, footed seafood cocktails, footed iced teas, footed fruit juices; height of goblet—6¼ in.; pattern includes 7½ and 8½ in. plates.

STEMWARE PATTERNS AND SHAPES

First row: (left to right) Duncan Rose on No. D8-1 shape, 6¾ in. goblet, 11 oz. capacity; Duncan Scroll on No. D5-1 shape, 6¼ in. goblet, 9 oz. capacity; Essex on No. D11-1 shape, 6 in. goblet, 10 oz. capacity; Garland on No. 5375-1 shape, 7 in. goblet, 9 oz. capacity. *Second row:* (left to right) Patio on No. D8-1 shape, 6¾ in. goblet, 11 oz. capacity; Platinum Band on No. D13-1 shape, 6½ in. goblet, 10 oz. capacity; Simplicity on No. D11-1 shape, 6 in. goblet, 10 oz. capacity.

1943 Catalogue. This factory catalogue showed the listings of crystal and glassware.

Duncan & Miller price sheet from 1951. Note the original price of the swans.

DUNCAN'S DECORATIVE & ACCESSORY CRYSTAL—Cont.
No. 30 Pattern

(Made in Crystal)

PALL MALL—Cont.

		LIST PRICE Dozen	Each
32/ 97	5½ in. Oval Ash Tray	$ 11.40	$ .95
32/ 98	7 in. Oval Ash Tray	18.00	1.50
32/100	4½ in. Oval Cigarette Box & Cover	24.00	2.00
30/101	4 in. Duck Ash Tray	18.00	1.50

CONDIMENT SETS

30/ 69	Salt (Metal Top)	$ 8.40	$ .70
30/ 70	Pepper (Metal Top)	8.40	.70
30/ 72	3 pc. Salt &— Pepper Set (Salt, Pepper, Tray)	24.00	2.00
30/ 73	3 oz. Oil w/Ground Stopper	27.00	2.25
30/ 75	3 pc. Oil & Vinegar Set (Oil, Vinegar, Tray)	60.00	5.00
30/ 76	5 pc. Condiment Set (Oil, Vinegar, Salt, Pepper, Tray)	75.00	6.25

TABLE ACCESSORIES

30/ 84	¼ lb. Butter & Cover	$ 36.00	$ 3.00
30/ 86	Syrup Pitcher 13 oz.	48.00	4.00
30/ 87	Sugar or Grated Cheese Shaker 13 oz.	42.00	3.50

DUNCAN SWANS

		Crystal, Green, Avocado or Teakwood LIST PRICE		Ruby LIST PRICE	
30/ 80	3½ in. Swan (12 to Ctn.)	$ 21.00	$ 1.75	$ 27.00	$ 2.25
30/ 81	7 in. Swan (12 to Ctn.)	27.00	2.25	33.00	2.75
30/ 82	10½ in. Swan (4 to Ctn.)	57.00	4.75	72.00	6.00
30/ 83	12 in. Swan (2 to Ctn.)	75.00	6.25	96.00	8.00

AMERICAN WAY
No. 71 Pattern

Made in Crystal

		LIST PRICE	
		Dozen	*Each*
76/ 28	14 in. Star Plate	$ 54.00	$ 4.50
78/ 59	15 in. Hors D'Oeuvres Tray 6 Compartment	60.00	5.00
72/106	13 in. Star Flower Bowl	54.00	4.50
72/116	8 in. Star Flared Vase	48.00	4.00
71/121	2 in. Star Candlestick	15.00	1.25

DUNCAN SPECIAL PIECES
Made in Crystal

		LIST PRICE	
		Dozen	*Each*
123/ 96	3 in. Clover Leaf Ash Tray	$ 6.00	$ .50
123/ 97	5 in. Clover Leaf Ash Tray	9.00	.75
123/ 98	6 in. Clover Leaf Ash Tray	21.00	1.75
538/103	3¼ in. Cigarette Holder	24.00	2.00
538/104	3 pc. Cigarette Set .... (Holder & 2-3½ Rect. Ash Trays)	36.00	3.00
121/117	14 in. Cornucopia Vase No. 2 Shape	60.00	5.00
529/118	7 in. Urn Vase Square Foot	39.00	3.25
530/119	7 in. Handled Urn Vase Square Foot ..	48.00	4.00
46/ 79	Muddler	10.80	.90
91/ 49	11 in. Celery Tray	30.00	2.50
118/ 80	10 in. Footed Salver	66.00	5.50
118/ 69	Salt (Metal Top)	8.40	.70
118/ 70	Pepper (Metal Top)	8.40	.70
118/ 71	3 pc. Salt & Pepper Set .... (Salt, Pepper, Tray)	24.00	2.00
	Duncan Three Face Comport with Cover ..	360.00	30.00
	Duncan Three Face Comport Only	240.00	20.00

1884 CATALOGUE

These pages are from the old catalogue of George Duncan & Sons. Very little has been written on the early Duncan and less illustrating the old glass made in Pittsburgh, Pennsylvania.

These early items are quite scarce, but that can be attributed to the fact that they are not recognized as Duncan. One fact that remains undisputed is that the glass was outstanding in beauty and quality.

Ruby glass was one of the most beautiful in color. This was obtained by dissolving a twenty-dollar gold piece in nitric and muriatic acid. This method ceased when Congress prohibited the destruction of United States coins, either silver or gold. As with time and knowledge, dyes came to replace the gold piece, so Duncan still retained its position in the field of fine glassware.

Other patterns which are not included in the 1884 catalogue are: Duncan Flute, No. 2004; Duncan Block, No. 326; Button Arches; Button Panel, No. 44; Grated Diamond and Sunburst, No. 20; Starred Loop, No. 45; Zippered Slash, No. 2005. These old patterns were popular around the turn of the century and are being eagerly sought by collectors today.

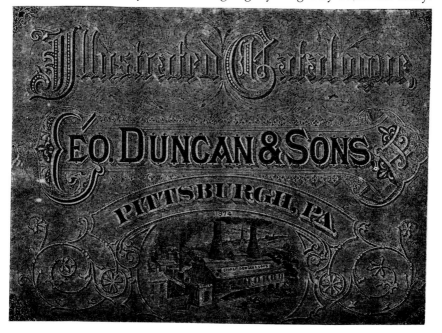

AMBERETTE STEMWARE

No. 48 Pattern

First row: (left to right) wine, engraving No. 536; claret, engraving No. 536; champagne, engraving No. 536; goblet, engraving No. 536; goblet, engraving No. 539; champagne, engraving No. 539; claret, engraving No. 539; wine, engraving No. 539. *Second row:* (left to right) goblet; champagne; claret; wine. (Also made in crystal)

AMBERETTE WARE

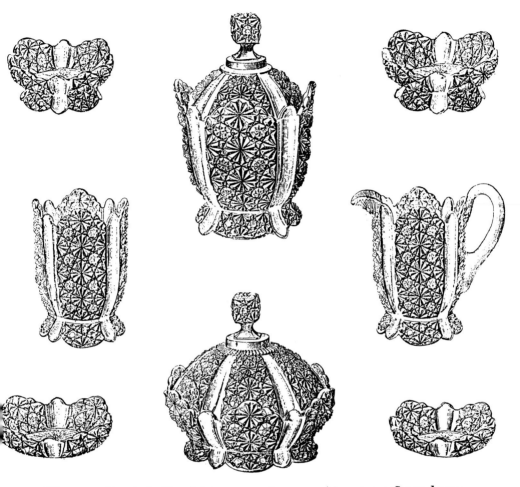

First row: (top to bottom) 4 in. comport; spoon; 4 in. nappy. *Second row:* (top and bottom) sugar; 8 in. butter and cover. *Third row:* (top to bottom) 4½ in. comport; cream; 4½ in. nappy.

NO. 230 ENGRAVING

No. 88 Pattern

First row: (left to right) butter and cover; cream; 4½ in. comport; 4 in. comport; (foreground) 4½ in. nappy. *Second row:* (left to right) spoon; sugar and cover; 4 in. nappy. *Third row:* (left to right) celery; qt. pitcher; ½ gal. pitcher.

NO. 230 ENGRAVING

No. 88 and No. 40 Patterns

First row: (left to right) No. 88 7 in. bowl; No. 40 cordial; No. 40 wine; No. 40 claret; No. 40 champagne; No. 40 goblet. *Second row:* (left and right) No. 88 8 in. bowl; No. 88 6 in. bowl. *Third row:* (left to right) No. 88 6 in. bowl and cover; No. 88 7 in. bowl and cover; No. 88 8 in. bowl and cover.

BAG WARE

First row: (left and right) octagonal rosette celery boat; finger bowl.
Second row: (left to right) spoon; (center) sugar and cover; cream.
Third row: (left to right) jelly or bowl; butter and cover; 4 in. comport.
(All items available in colors)

First row: (left to right) 9 in. orange bowl; celery; 8 in. orange bowl. *Second row:* (left to right) 7 in. bowl and cover, available in 8 in. size; catsup, pressed or cut stopper; 7 in. bowl, uncovered, available in 8 in. size.

BAG WARE

Additional items made in this pattern were: 8 in. wide, 5½ in. deep orange bowl; 9 in. wide, 6 in. deep orange bowl; catsup bottle, 6½ in. measuring from lip of bottle to base, stopper 2½ in. cut or pressed—not included in measurement of bottle; celery, 6 in. high; pitchers, 3 pt.,— 6 in. high, 1 qt.—5 in. high, 1 gal.—7 in. high; 7, 8, and 10 in. shallow bowls. George Duncan & Sons also made a 7 or 8 in. bowl that could be bought with or without a cover. When the lid was placed on the bowl, it added an additional five inches to the height.

BAR TUMBLERS

First row: (left and right corners) pillar toy; Barney toy. *Second row:* (left to right) No. 28 4¾ oz.; No. 29 3¾ oz.; No. 30 5 oz.; No. 31 sham; No. 34 5 oz.; No. 35; No. 37 5 oz.; No. 38 3½ oz.; No. 39 5½ oz.; No. 40 5½ oz.; No. 41 5¼ oz. *Third row:* (left to right) No. 82 2 oz.; No. 83 2 oz.; No. 84 3 oz., sham sides; No. 85 2½ oz. sham; No. 86 4 oz.; No. 45 4½ oz.; No. 46 4¾ oz. sham; No. 47 4 oz.; No. 48 3½ oz. sham; No. 49 5 oz. *Fourth row:* (left to right) No. 46 2¾ oz.; No. 92 3 oz.; No. 91 2½ oz.; No. 44 4 oz.. *Fifth row:* (left to right) No. 61; No. 34 5 oz., No. 0 engraving; No. 49 5 oz., No. 0 engraving; No. 34 5 oz., No. 59 engraving; 3½ oz. Gill Jose; 3 oz. Irish; No. 60; 2½ oz. Gill jigger; 3 oz. Gill plain sham; No. 75 2 oz.; No. 87 2½ oz. sham. *Sixth row:* (left to right) No. 77 8 oz.; No. 78 8½ oz.; No. 79 10 oz.; No. 80 6½ oz.; No. 63 4 oz.; No. 76 3½ oz.; No. 60 4¼ oz.; No. 62 6½ oz.; No. 64 6 oz.

BLOWN WATER SETS

Left: No. 33/4 pitcher, engraving No. 433; X5 tumbler, engraving No. 433; X finger bowl, engraving No. 433; No. 800 wine or water tray. *Right:* No. 33/4 pitcher, engraving No. 427; X5 tumbler, engraving No. 427; X finger bowl, engraving No. 427; No. 800 wine or water tray. *Center:* No. 33/3 pitcher, engraving No. 434; X5 tumbler, engraving No. 434; X finger bowl, engraving No. 434; No. 800 wine or water tray.

DECANTERS, WATER, BAR, AND BITTER BOTTLES

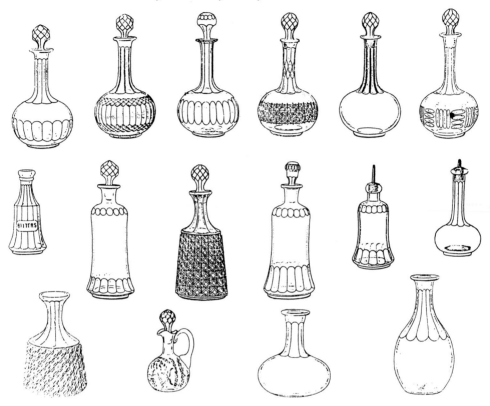

First row: (left to right) No. 1 decanter, cut No. 8; No. 1 decanter, cut No. 14; No. 1 decanter, cut No. 15; No. 1 decanter, cut No. 6; No. 1 decanter, cut No. 5; No. 1 decanter, cut No. 7. *Second row:* (left to right) bitter bottle; No. 3 bar bottle; No. 800 decanter; No. bar bottle; No. 1 bitter and tube; No. 3 bitter and tube. *Third row:* (left to right) No. 800 water bottle; No. 1 vinegar, plain, bottle engraved; No. 2 water bottle, cut neck; No. 3 water bottle, cut neck and star bottom.

Ellrose Ware

First row: (left to right) 9 in. gas shade; 10 in. salver; celery. *Second row:* (left to right) ½ gal. pitcher; tumbler; qt. pitcher. (All items available in colors)

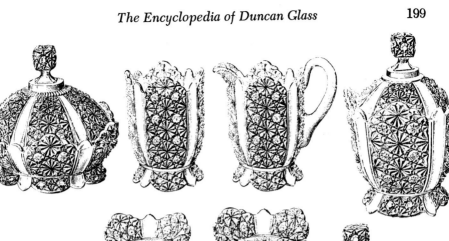

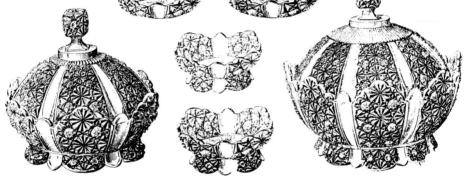

First row: (left to right) 6 in. butter and cover; spoon; cream; sugar.
Second row: (left and right) 4 in. nappy; 4½ in. nappy. *Third row:* (left
to right) 7 in. comport and cover; (background) 4 in. comport; 4½ in.
comport; 8 in. comport and cover. (All items available in colors)

ELLROSE WARE

The following items were available in this pattern: 7, 8, and 9 in. footed oval bowls; 7, 8, and 9 in. nappys; 8 in. round bowl, also available flared; 9 in. round bowl, also available flared; 5 in. Berry nappy; 6 in. olive dish; 11½ in. by 9 in. bread plate; 7 in. plate; 7 in. comport, 3 in. tall; 8 in. comport, 4 in. tall; 7 in. goblet. (The 8 and 9 in. round and flared bowls were made with a foot.)

ENGRAVED STEMWARE

First row: (left to right) No. 41 goblet, engraving No. 400; No. 41 champagne, engraving No. 400; No. 41 claret, engraving No. 400; No. 41 wine, engraving No. 400; No. 41 cordial, engraving No. 400; No. 44 wine, engraving No. 447; No. 44 claret, engraving No. 447; No. 44 champagne, engraving No. 447; No. 44 goblet, engraving No. 436. *Second row:* (left to right) No. 32 goblet, engraving No. 00; No. 4 Mitchell goblet, engraving No. 393; No. 45 goblet, engraving No. 00; No. 1 Mitchell goblet, engraving No. 3; No. 7 Mitchell goblet, engraving No. 10; No. 7 Mitchell goblet, engraving No. 13; No. 25 plain goblet, engraving No. 53; No. 24 goblet, engraving No. 60. *Third row:* (left to right) No. 2 Mitchell goblet, engraving No. 394; 4 in. Mitchell goblet, engraving No. 227; No. 25 goblet, engraving No. 208; No. 28 goblet, engraving No. 136; No. 31 goblet, engraving No. 389; No. 32 goblet, engraving No. 385; No. 41 goblet, engraving No. 387; No. 41 goblet, engraving No. 391. *Fourth row:* (left to right) No. 2 plain goblet, engraving No. 384; No. 31 goblet, engraving No. 235; No. 319 goblet, engraving No. 383; No. 39 goblet, engraving No. 386; No. 40 goblet, engraving No. 385½; No. 41 goblet, engraving No. 382; No. 45 goblet, engraving No. 441; No. 415 goblet, engraving No. 390.

GLASS NOVELTIES

George Duncan & Sons was well known for glass novelties. One such item was a matchbox made in the shape of a bale of cotton, measuring 3¼ in. long and 2 in. deep. It could also be used for a small candy box.

Open top hats were made in four sizes, and they looked like a hat turned upside down. The hats were made in both crystal and colors. The 1¼ in. high size was used for individual salt; the 2 in. size was a toothpick holder; the 3 in. size a spoon holder; and the 4¼ in. size a celery holder.

They also made an umbrella-shaped vase with a foot. This vase measured 6¼ in. tall, including the handle, which was made of metal. Some were made without the foot.

A glass chair, a little German band cap, a lady's slipper, and a 4½ in. sled were among other items produced by George Duncan & Sons.

The slipper, the top hats, and the umbrella (see illustrations) appear to be in the same pattern, which is called Hobnail under the illustration of their slipper as shown in their 1884 catalogue. In this old book were other bowls listed as Hobnail, although the pattern shown was later called Daisy and Button.

First row: (left to right) individual hat salt; hat toothpick; hat spoon; hat celery. *Second row:* (left to right) little German band cap; chair; cotton bale matchbox. *Third row:* (left and right) Hobnail slipper; footed umbrella.

GLASSWARE

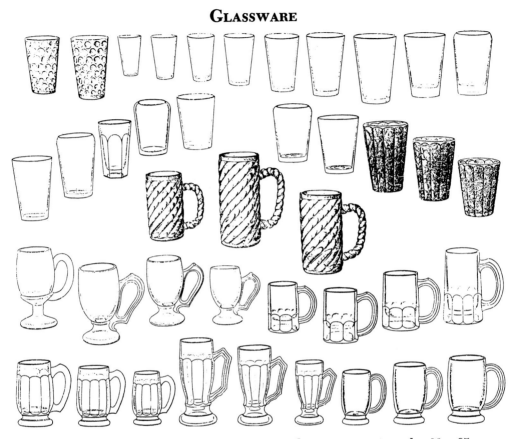

First row: (left to right) 10 oz. optic soda; 13 oz. optic soda; No. 65 2½ oz.; No. 66 3½ oz.; No. 67 4½ oz.; No. 68 6½ oz.; No. 69 10 oz.; No. 70 13 oz.; No. 71 18 oz.; No. 1 12 oz. soda; No. 1 12 oz. cupped soda. *Second row:* (left to right) 13 oz. plain lemonade; 13 oz. plain, cupped lemonade; No. 6 flute soda; No. 2 10 oz. cupped soda; No. 2 10 oz. soda; 12 oz. cupped soda; 12 oz. soda; No. 555 18 oz. soda; No. 555 13 oz. soda; No. 555 12 oz. tumbler. *Third row:* (center, left to right) No. 60 5 oz. pony beer; No. 62 large beer; No. 61 medium beer. *Fourth row:* (left to right) No. 6 10 oz. footed lager; No. 5 8 oz. large lager; No. 5 7 oz. medium lager; No. 5 5 oz. pony lager; 5 oz. pony St. Louis; 7 oz. medium St. Louis; 8 oz. large St. Louis; 10 oz. extra large St. Louis. *Fifth row:* (left to right) 8 oz. large Miller; 7 oz. medium Miller; 5 oz. pony Miller; No. 76 8 oz. large mug; No. 76 6½ oz. medium mug; No. 76 pony mug; plain pony mug; plain medium mug; plain large mug.

First row: (left to right) 4 oz. flared Mitchell pony ale; 5 oz. flared medium Mitchell ale; 7 oz. flared large Mitchell ale; 7¼ oz. flared, optic large Mitchell ale; 5¼ oz. flared, optic medium Mitchell ale; 4¼ oz. flared optic pony Mitchell ale; 7 oz. large Mitchell ale; 5 oz. medium Mitchell ale; 4 oz. pony Mitchell ale; No. 55 9½ oz.; No. 54 5 oz.; No. 56 6½ oz. ale. *Second row:* (left to right) No. 59 10 oz. large ale; No. 58 8 oz. medium ale; No. 57 5 oz. pony ale; No. 61 4½ oz. bottle beer; No. 63 4 oz. bottle beer; No. 40 large ale; Yorkshire ale; No. 51 6 oz.; No. 52 8 oz.; No. 53 11 oz.; No. 46 7½ oz. large ale; No. 46 5½ oz. ale; No. 46 3½ oz. ale; (background) No. 40 pony ale; 9 oz. Tyrrell ale; 8 oz. medium Tyrrell ale; 5½ oz. plain pony. *Third row:* (left to right) No. 32 7½ oz. straight large ale; No. 32 6 oz. straight medium ale; No. 32 3½ oz. straight pony ale; No. 32 flared pony ale; No. 32 6 oz. flared medium ale; No. 32 7½ oz. flared large ale; No. 100 10 oz. footed beer; No. 100 10 oz. flared footed beer; 14 oz. English schooner; 18 oz. Mitchell flared schooner; 18 oz. Mitchell straight schooner.

GOBLETS

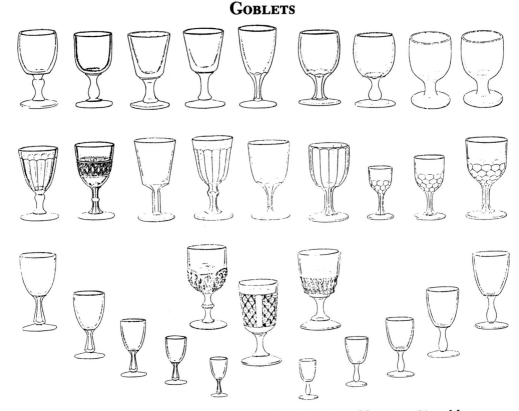

First row: (left to right) No. 10 goblet; No. 18 goblet; No. 19 goblet; No. 24 goblet; No. 29 goblet; Leland hotel goblet; No. 1 plain or hotel goblet; No. 43 goblet; No. 46 goblet. *Second row:* (left to right) No. 13 goblet; No. 14 goblet; No. 35 goblet; No. 36 goblet; No. 37 goblet; Huber goblet; No. 15 wine; No. 15 champagne; No. 15 goblet. *Third row:* (center, left to right) No. 555 goblet; No. 65 goblet; No. 600 goblet. *Fourth row:* (left to right) No. 5 plain goblet; No. 5 plain champagne; No. 5 plain claret; No. 5 plain cordial; No. 2 plain cordial; No. 2 plain wine; No. 2 plain claret; No. 2 plain champagne; No. 2 plain goblet.

First row: (left to right) ½ pt. saloon; ½ pt. plain, heavy; ½ pt. plain, light; No. 2 plain punty; ½ pt. Chicago; ½ pt. Cuba punty; Fifth Avenue; ⅓ qt. Gem; ⅓ qt. Huber. *Second row:* (left to right) No. 51; No. 52; No. 53; No. 54; No. 55; ½ pt. flute punty. *Third row:* (left to right) No. 301 8 oz. tumbler; No. 302 8½ oz. tumbler; No. 303 tumbler; No. 304 tumbler; No. 306 tumbler; No. 72; No. 73; No. 74. *Fourth row:* (left to right) No. 300 8½ oz. tumbler; No. 52, engraving No. 106; No. 52, engraving No. 110; No. 51, engraving No. 107; ½ pt. plain tumbler, light, engraving No. 0; No. 555 9 oz. table; No. 56 bar. *Fifth row:* (left to right) ½ pt. Cate; ⅓ pt. Star; ½ pt. Star; No. 81 tumbler; ⅓ pt. square jelly; ½ pt. square jelly; ⅓ pt. jelly; ½ pt. jelly.

LAMPS

First row: (left and right) No. 12 9 in. lamp, also available in 8 in. size
(No. 11), and 7 in. size (No. 10); No. 20 9 in. lamp, also available in
8 in. size (No. 19), and 7 in. size (No. 18). *Second row:* (left and right)
No. 16 9 in. lamp, also available in 8 in. size (No. 15), and 7 in. size
(No. 14); No. 22 2-handled lamp, also available in 2½ in. size (No. 23),
and 2 in. size (No. 22).

EXTRA HEAVY PRESSED LAMPS

No. 850 Pattern

First row: (left to right) No. 2 2-handled lamp; No. 3 2-handled lamp; No. 4 2-handled lamp; No. 5 2-handled lamp; No. 6 2-handled lamp; No. 7 2-handled lamp; No. 1 2-handled lamp; 1-handled lamp. *Second row:* (left to right) No. 24 lamp; No. 25 lamp; No. 26 lamp; No. 27 2-collar lamp.

MITCHELL STEMWARE

Supposedly the first ware made by the Duncan & Miller Glass Company when the plant started operation in Washington, Pennsylvania on February 9, 1893, several items were found in the plant, before the fire in 1956. These are highly prized today. One of the pieces found was the No. 2 shape and believed to be a wine. There are many different shapes, but they are all listed under one name.

First row: (left to right) No. 1 goblet; No. 1 champagne; No. 1 claret; No. 1 wine; No. 1 cordial; No. 2 cordial; No. 2 wine; No. 2 claret; No. 2 champagne; No. 2 goblet. *Second row:* (left to right) No. 3 goblet; No. 3· champagne; No. 3 claret; No. 3 wine; No. 4 cordial; No. 4 wine; No. 4 claret; No. 4 champagne; No. 4 goblet. *Third row:* (left to right) No. 7 goblet; No. 7 champagne; No. 7 claret; No. 7 wine; No. 3 cocktail; No. 415 cordial; No. 415 wine; No. 415 wine; No. 415 champagne; No. 415 goblet.

This photo of Mitchell Stemware is *not* taken from the original 1884 catalogue.

No. 800 Pattern

First row: (left to right) table salt; salt or pepper bottle; mustard; individual salt; 4½ in. sled; 4 in. comport; No. 800½ pepper bottle with plated top; No. 800½ mustard with plated top; No. 800½ salt bottle with plated top. *Second row:* (left to right) 11 in. celery boat; 6 in. flanged butter; 4½ in. Berry nappy; (foreground) 5 in. ice cream nappy; 4 in. nappy; 4½ in. nappy; pickle boat. *Third row:* (left to right) oil or vinegar bottle; goblet; 9½ oz. goblet; 6½ oz. champagne; 4¼ oz. claret; 2½ oz. wine; 1 oz. cordial; table tumbler; pt. mal carafe. *Fourth row:* (left to right) cheese plate and cover; ½ gal. tankard; ½ gal. pitcher; celery; cheese plate and cover. Name—Heavy paneled fine cut.

No. 1003 Ware

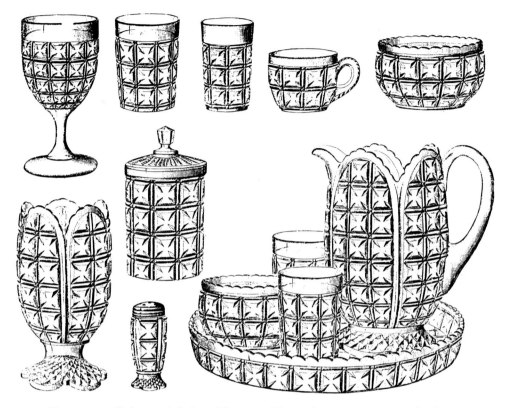

First row: (left to right) goblet; tumbler; champagne; custard; finger bowl. *Second row:* (left to right) celery; salt bottle; (background) pickle jar; wine tray.

First row: (left to right) 4 in. comport; butter; 4½ in. comport. *Second row:* (left and right) spoon; cream. *Third row:* (left to right) 7 in. Berry nappy; sugar; 8 in. Berry nappy.

First row: (left to right) 7 in. plate; 5 in. plate; 10 in. salver; pickle boat.
Second row: (left to right) 8 in. comport; crumb plate; 7 in. comport.

No. 1003 Ware

Items made in this pattern included: 12 in. round wine tray; 11 in. by 9 in. bread tray; 15 in. by 9 in. oblong ice cream tray; 11 in. by ½ in. oval celery boot; 7, 8, and 9 in. long oval dishes; 8 in. water bottle; oil bottle, 5 in. from lip to base, stopper measures 2 additional inches in height; 9½ in. brandy bottle, stopper measures 3 additional inches; 7, 8, and 9 in. orange bowls, 5 in. deep, with crystal scallops making a striking effect as they separate the block design clear to the base, almost in the same way an orange would be after it has been peeled (small nappys also made this way); 9 in. round Berry nappy with matching small bowls; ½ gal. water pitcher. The name Maltese Cross was given to this pattern and was patented in 1886.

POLKA DOT WARE

No. 47 Pattern

First row: (left to right) sugar; 4 in. nappy; celery; 4 in. comport; 5 in. bowl. *Second row:* (left to right) cream; spoon; 6 in. bowl; 7 in. bowl, without cover. *Third row:* (left to right) 6 in. butter and cover; 8 in. bowl, without cover; 9 in. bowl, without cover. *Fourth row:* (left to right) qt. pitcher; ½ gal. pitcher; 7 in. bowl and cover; 8 in. bowl and cover; 9 in. bowl and cover.

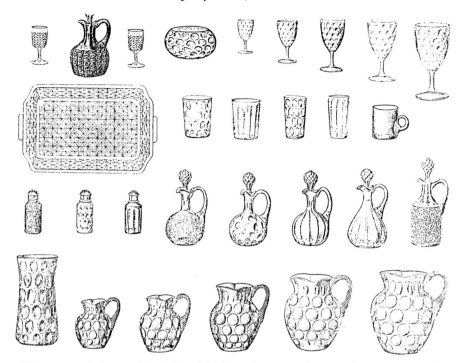

First row: (left to right) No. 800 brandy set and tray (below); No. 2 Polka Dot; Polka Dot cordial; Polka Dot wine; Polka Dot claret; Polka Dot champagne; Polka Dot goblet. *Second row:* (left to right) No. 800 brandy tray (part of set); Polka Dot tumbler; optic tumbler; Polka Dot champagne; optic champagne; No. 44 lemonade. *Third row:* (left to right) Craquelled individual salt bottle; Polka Dot individual salt bottle; optic individual salt bottle; No. 1 Craquelled oil or vinegar bottle; No. 1 Polka Dot oil or vinegar bottle; No. 1 optic oil or vinegar bottle; No. 3 optic oil or vinegar bottle; octagonal rosette oil and vinegar. *Fourth row:* (left to right) Polka Dot celery, blown; No. 34½ Polka Dot; No. 34-1 Polka Dot; No. 34-2 Polka Dot; No. 34-4 Polka Dot; No. 34-5 Polka Dot.

SALVERS

First row: (left to right) 8 in. solid stem; 9 in. solid stem; 10 in. solid stem; 12 in. solid stem. *Second row:* (left to right) No. 800 8 in. salver; No. 400 9 in. salver; No. 400 11 in. salver. *Third row:* (left to right) No. 800 10 in. salver; No. 800 9 in. salver; No. 400 10 in. salver.

STEMWARE

First row: (left to right) No. 39 goblet, engraving No. 259; No. 39 champagne, engraving No. 259; No. 39 claret, engraving No. 259; No. 39 wine, engraving No. 259; No. 39 cordial, engraving No. 259; No. 39 cordial, engraving No. 303; No. 39 wine, engraving No. 303; No. 39 claret, engraving No. 303; No. 39 champagne, engraving No. 303; No. 39 goblet, engraving No. 303. *Second row:* (left to right) No. 37 goblet, engraving No. 210½; No. 31 champagne, engraving No. 210½; No. 31 claret, engraving No. 210½; No. 31 wine, engraving No. 210½; No. 31 cordial, engraving No. 210½; No. 32 cordial, engraving No. 230; No. 32 wine, engraving No. 230; No. 32 claret, engraving No. 230; No. 32 champagne, engraving No. 230; No. 32 goblet, engraving No. 230. *Third row:* (left to right) No. 32 goblet, engraving No. 272; No. 32 champagne, engraving No. 272; No. 32 claret, engraving No. 272; No. 32 claret, engraving No. 272; No. 32 cordial, engraving No. 272; No. 25 cordial, engraving No. 263; No. 25 claret, engraving No. 263; No. 25 champagne, engraving No. 263; No. 25 goblet, engraving No. 263. *Fourth row:* (left to right) No. 7 goblet, engraving No. 218; No. 7 champagne, engraving No. 218; No. 7 claret, engraving No. 218; No. 7 wine, engraving No. 218.

First row: (left to right) No. 1 1 oz. sherry; No. 1 1 oz. flared sherry; No. 2 1½ oz. sherry; No. 2 1½ oz. flared sherry; No. 3 sherry; ¾ oz. Hennesey brandy; 2½ oz. Mitchell cocktail; No. 2 2½ oz. flared cocktail; No. 7 2½ oz. flared cocktail; No. 7 2½ oz. cocktail. *Second row:* (left to right) No. 8 3½ oz. cocktail; No. 9 4 oz. saucer champagne; No. 10 8 oz. cocktail; No. 10 8 oz. flared cocktail; No. 11 8 oz. cocktail; No. 12 2½ oz. cocktail; No. 13 3 oz. cocktail; No. 14 cocktail. *Third row:* (left to right) No. 29, engraved; Bristow champagne, hollow stem; No. 10 3½ oz. champagne, hollow stem; No. 11 champagne; No. 4 3¼ oz. Mitchell saucer champagne; No. 34 4 oz. wine; No. 42 4 oz. wine; No. 40 3 oz. cocktail. *Fourth row:* (left to right) No. 3 5 oz. cupped hot whiskey; No. 2 plain hot whiskey; No. 4 5 oz. flared hot whiskey; No. 44 3 oz. wine; No. 44 4½ oz. claret; flared Mitchell Catawba; Mitchell Catawba.

First row: (left to right) No. 40 goblet; No. 40 champagne; No. 40 claret; No. 40 wine; No. 40 cordial; No. 39 cordial; No. 39 wine; No. 39 claret; No. 39 champagne; No. 39 goblet. *Second row:* (left to right) No. 31 goblet; No. 31 champagne; No. 31 claret; No. 31 wine; No. 32 wine; No. 32 claret; No. 32 champagne; No. 32 goblet. *Third row:* (left to right) No. 17 goblet; No. 17 champagne; No. 17 claret; No. 17 wine; No. 19 wine; No. 19 claret; No. 19 champagne; No. 19 goblet.

TOILET SETS

First row: (left and right) No. 5 cologne bottle (also available in 16 oz. size)—8 in. tall without stopper, 8 oz. size—6 in., 6 oz. size—5 in., 4 oz. size—4 in., 2 oz. size—3 in., 1 oz. size—2 in.; No. 2 cologne bottle with No. 380 engraving. *Second row:* (left to right) octagonal powder bottle box (also made with matching perfume box); No. 2 cologne bottle, No. 381 engraving; No. 1 puff box (also made in matching cologne bottles).

WINE AND BRANDY SETS

First row: (left to right) No. 2 engraved wine set; No. 800 wine set with cut or pressed stopper; No. 3 engraved wine set. *Second row:* (left to right) No. 6 engraved wine set (tray in foreground); No. 1 brandy set (cut decanter and blown optic tumblers); No. 5 engraved wine set (tray in foreground).